Mary.
With love en
gift is given, in you joy
Marcus xxx

THE CONTRADICTIONS OF LIFE

NAVIGATING YOUR PATH TO PERSONAL FREEDOM

By

Marcus James

ISBN-978-0-9568403-2-5

THE CONTRADICTIONS OF LIFE

NAVIGATING YOUR PATH TO PERSONAL FREEDOM

By

Marcus James

ACKNOWLEDGMENTS

***

To Neale Donald Walsch
I sincerely thank my friend and mentor,
for your encouragement and words of wisdom.
Your kindness to me fills my heart brother;
I surely repay you with my love and gratitude.

***

To Jami Lynn Sands
You have a skill, patience, a gift, and a willingness that I
admire, appreciate and value. Thank you for sharing your
editing talents and for walking this journey with me.

***

To all those I have met while walking this path called life; those
who have encouraged me, and those who tried to silence me;
without each one of you I would not be where I am today.

TABLE OF CONTENTS

FOREWARD

Isn't this an interesting experience, this thing called life? Here
we all are, most of us several (if not many) years into it, and
we're still talking about it as if we have no understanding of it at
all – or as if we understand it completely, or as if both are true.
In fact, that is what is so, unless it is not. It surely is for me.

One day I understand life completely, utterly, and absolutely,
and the next day I realize that I have barely touched the surface
of it; that there is so much more to know, that for me to imagine
that I understand it completely is simply absurd. Except that I do
understand it completely… including my complete
understanding that I cannot understand it completely.

Do you understand? If you do, you are ready for this book. If
you don't, you are even more ready.

In this remarkable volume, Marcus James McKeown offers a
wonderfully simple look at the complexities of life, using
explanations so complete that they render each topic simple to
master. This is the veritable handbook for life itself, clarifying
exactly what's going on in a way that unravels life's mysteries
while keeping the magic of life intact.

To twist a phrase from Shakespeare, 'tis a contradiction
devoutly to be wished'.

Ah, yes… to know life so well that the not knowing what's next
becomes what is excitedly expected; to place at the edge of
surprise, at the border of delight, even as we distance ourselves
from the fear of the unknown. This is truly living. The manual

you are holding in your hand is a map sure and true, leading you to the 'Land of Discovering the Already Discovered'.

What a glorious contradiction!

Although every now and then I found a statement that does not align with my personal understanding, not all of the views expressed here need to be in accordance with my own for me to invite you to this exploration. I believe you will find it valuable as an igniter of your own thought process on some important life experiences.

Enjoy the read... you may well find yourself encountering for the first time some of what you have known forever.

NEALE DONALD WALCH
Author of 'Conversations with God'

INTRODUCTION

Your life's journey has brought you to this book. Why?

The path of life is filled with contradictions. Some are relatively easy to grasp and figure out, but others present us with near impossible contradictory realities, i.e. two truths equally as powerful, but each one delivering a complete opposite reality, and each one true, and unquestionable in that truth. Perhaps just one paragraph, one line, or one word within these pages will resonate with you. Perhaps it will send a flash of insight straight to your consciousness that you will observe as everything changes. Speaking from experience, if you can get the underlying message that is hidden within the pages of this book, everything will change; it must.

Here in part, is how this book came into being: I was driving on a road south of Mexico City that twisted and wormed its way around the mountain side. To my amazement, as I looked out the window, I became aware that each side of the mountain was completely different from the next; one side was mostly desert-like and another was covered with flowers in bloom. Still another side was simply standing tall and showing its age by presenting trees that had surely outlived the planets oldest human inhabitants.
A seemingly normal moment was interrupted by an inner experience of knowing and awareness. I began to hear gentle voices within say; 'the same and different', 'one reality, many faces', 'one mound, many mountains', 'one book, many stories'.

Before I knew what was going on, I could see generations of time and change flashing before my eyes and speaking to my soul. I began to see the mountain in a way I could never have imagined. It became alive in a way that left me speechless and experiencing an internal bliss. I was overwhelmed by the connection I felt to life in that moment, and the message the mountain brought to me that day.

So it is with this book and the messages written into its pages. It is possible to read through the words and not even know there is a gift for you. Furthermore, there are many gifts. If you read through the pages with the intention to see, an openness to allow, and an agreement to suspend current beliefs and judgments, you will see the mountain as the mountain truly stands, and not as you have seen it in other times you passed by.

I will point out the first gift and you can sit back and allow the countless others to rise up and show themselves, as you are ready to see them. The first gift--this book was written for you and you alone. It is not a book that was written for just anyone; no it was written for you. I knew you even before I began scribbling the first words. Yes, you are the reason for its being. The messages and hints about life that you will come across in this book are for you and you alone. Do not feel the need to accept or reject this first gift, just allow it to be, and enter this moment with a sense of acceptance. As you see and experience the other gifts that are waiting for you, you will begin to realize that this book really was written for you and no one else. Imagine, an entire book written, edited, re-edited, published, distributed, promoted and positioned throughout the world, just so you could find it, read it and connect with the opportunity it offers you to see things as they really are; just so you could find what you have been seeking. What is it like to hear that? Do you dismiss it right away? Are you that resistant to letting in some love and attention, or are you willing to not judge it and wait and see what happens?

The very act of writing this down was an incredible experience for me. From start to finish, the first draft was written in twenty-one days. However, it did not happen in the space of three weeks; it was spread out over a period of eighteen months. When it felt right I would type a little, and if it didn't feel right, I simply didn't. I have learned to live my life in accordance with my gut feeling. Whenever I lose sight or become upset, worried, fearful, or unsure, it is because I have stopped listening to my heart and instinct, and started listening to my head again. When I refer to my 'gut', I am not talking about my feeling or my deep down sense of what is or is not. I am talking about the absolute knowing, the unquestionable truth, and the voice of self that gets it right, because there is no other option but to get it right. I am referring to the experience of listening to 'Spirit', hearing God, and dancing with the energy that is life itself. One of the other gifts you may find here is how you access that ability for yourself. The 'how' is here, written for you, and waiting for you to discover it...

Contradiction # 1

Uncertainty Is The
Only Certainty

It is true that there is nothing certain in life other than uncertainty itself, which in effect, tells us that it is possible to find certainty. The only catch is that the certainty you are seeking is not necessarily the certainty you will find. While this may seem confusing, go deeper to consider that uncertainty is the only real expression of certainty available to you, unless it's not.

We have become deeply programmed to believe that we can control, order and manage life to the point of being able to determine everything. We seem to spend a vast amount of time seeking out the experience of this programming, and for what? In the end, we find that life seems to have its own idea of the way things are, the way things can be, and the way things will be. So why bother? What is it that drives us all to the point of madness, trying to find something that is not there to be found? Why do we continually choose to believe that we can make what is already perfect even more perfect? What are the voices within us that seem to have the power to make us believe that even though everything in the world tells us that the search for certainty is a fool's search, we still manage to find a way to ignore them and look for it anyway.

Nothing is certain. It is not certain that you will make it home today, it is not certain that your children will live longer than you, it is not certain that you will manage to keep up your mortgage payments, it is not certain that you will die having fulfilled your life's purpose, and it is certainly not certain that you will make sense of this thing called 'life'. So what is the point?

There is a Point
Depending on the way you were trained, programmed and ordered to engage in life, you can find yourself either in a place of freedom where everything seems to be okay most of the time, or where everything seems to be a struggle and a challenge all of the time. The odd exception being when, for some unknown reason, something goes right.

We invest so much energy trying to figure life out, nail it down and mold it into what we believe it should look like. Of course, the issue here is not what you are doing or trying to do. The issue is what you believe and how you are living your life in accordance with those beliefs. Take a moment to reflect on this -- you only know what you know, and there is much that you do not yet know. Considering that there is much you do not know, how can you claim to know the way life should be? Or claim to know how life can be manipulated into what you think it should

13

be? You can only know the way life can be in accordance with the map you have of life, and in accordance with the knowledge you have been given. Furthermore, what about all the other maps and the knowledge the rest of the people in the world are accessing? Many of these are different than your version, and they tell a different story than the story you have been living with. Are we to suggest that you are right and they are wrong, or perhaps they are right and you are wrong? Maybe there is another option, do you think it is possible that neither are right or wrong, and in fact, we are all just bringing different pieces of the puzzle to the table?

Who taught you what you know, and where did they get their information? It seems that we get to a point in life where we stop learning, and start to think that we have enough knowledge to know how to handle all situations, but then what? We get a job, earn some money, buy a house, and enter a contract to repay the bank big sums of money for twenty-five years. We may even have a few children. Whenever possible, we escape the madness of the world of certainty, for a holiday that allows us to convince ourselves that it is all worthwhile. This seems to be what makes sense and lets us feel that we are on the right path; after all, that is the norm.

While we are having this experience, we go to our counselor, our psychotherapist, our doctor, the pharmacy, and the life coach to try to figure out what has gone wrong. Somehow, we don't feel the pay off that we imagined would be waiting for us.

Nor do we feel the benefit or the rest that should come with having everything so right and in place.

It seems that we have a number of options, but there are two in particular worth looking at. The first option is to live as if you are 'God'. In this scenario, you believe that it is up to you to manage everything, be responsible for everything, control everything, and be the one that makes it all happen. In this delusion, you feel that if it were not for you, everything and everyone around you would be lost and running through the world like headless chickens. This option will drive you crazy in short order. Option number two is very different; to live a life knowing that you are indeed God, and to act as God does. Allowing everything to be exactly as it is, and knowing that it is perfect, just the way it is. You see the connection in everything and know that nothing is without reason. You accept all events and situations as a part of the ultimate plan and the true purpose of life, knowing that nothing needs changing. Why would something that is perfect need to change if it's already perfect?

Is there a flaw
The only flaw there is in the tapestry of life is the flaw that you choose to see. This is done by looking at life through a filter system that has been created by those who taught you how to see things the way you do.

Everything is what it is, and doesn't need to be anything else. The problem is not that there is a flaw; the problem is that you believe there is a flaw. Somehow you feel you need to fix it, make it better, perfect it, and put a shine on it where no shine needed.

Nothing is wrong with anything, everything is perfect, everything has all of the shine it needs. If it needed a better shine, it would have it. Nothing needs you to fix it; you have to understand, see, believe, and experience that, so you can know how to let go, and enjoy the perfection that is in everything.

Leave it in its natural state

Considering that everything is perfect just as it is, we can easily conclude that the flaw we see in it is simply our impression of it. Since we do not know everything there is to know, we can conclude that we are very possibly making a judgement that is affecting not only how we see things, but also how we experience them. This stands to reason, given the fact that we usually experience things in a way that supports how we see them.

The challenge for you may be the fact that you really can see how things could be made better or fixed, and because of that you get busy attempting to change them. When you start changing things, you upset the natural process of the things you are changing. The result of this is what makes them flawed, and this in turn demands you do something to fix them. So in effect, we move the natural order of things in such a way that we justify our belief that they need to be rearranged, moved around, or fixed. In this way, we create a comfort in knowing that we are doing the right thing, by putting right the things that have gone wrong. The great challenge we are faced with, in terms of moving beyond the need to change what is already perfect, is to leave everything as it is. If you find that the situation you are in is one that needs fixing, changing or manipulating, it is most likely because you have not allowed your life to be what it is intended to be. Instead you have redirected it, thereby creating the flaw, instead of the flow, that needs to be 'unflawed'.

The objective is to allow the natural state of things to re-enter the equation. For this to happen, you simply need to do nothing. Nature will enter again, once that which keeps pushing it out stops pushing it out.

Nature is the teacher

Watch the seasons as they pass, and you will see the greatest teacher you could ever find, as she works her magic. Not a manager, not a director, not a leadership team, nor strategic plan in sight, and yet everything works out beautifully. When it is time; not a minute too late or a minute too early, the fields are rich with color, the trees are complete with flowering seeds and the crops that feed us; they spring up to offer themselves as a rich bounty. When it is time to sleep, everything simply turns itself inwards for a season of rest, in preparation for what is soon to be again.

The only thing you will see in nature is the beauty, the perfect dance, and the immaculate perfection of certainty that lives in uncertainty. There are no guarantees in nature; the tree that stands tall this year may be lying flat at the bottom of a hill next year, the roses that make you smile this season will never return, but their place will be filled with more beauty next season. The crop

17

that feeds you will leave behind the seeds of what will feed you next year. It is a journey of never knowing and always knowing. What allows this dance to happen is the power of nature to do its own thing in its own way. When there is no interference in the natural order of things, balance is certain, but that certainty depends on the uncertainty in order to allow that birth to happen.

The Tyranny of Security

Underlying the 'if only I could make it right' myth, is the need for security; to know that everything is safe with little or no risk; that I am insulated against anything that might threaten my reality. Many of us over invest in chasing this security. We convince ourselves that having that well paid job with the right pension provision and health benefits will insulate us from financial threats. We erroneously believe that with no financial threat, we will be happier. Ask yourself this question: Am I willing to stay with a job (or any life situation), even though I am not happy, rather than take a risk in searching for something that will give me fulfilment? Incredibly, we have allowed ourselves to be misled into believing that a job with a good salary that covers our needs, and offers us security, means that life is working out okay. If we go deeper into that feeling, we will realize we are not being truthful with ourselves. A good job with a salary that covers the bills does not provide you with security, it simply pays the bills.

Security, in the real sense of the word, is something totally different. Real security is something that offers a knowledge of self, a feeling of value, an understanding of belonging, an experience of confidence, and an expression of connectedness. The real joy in it, however, is that it is something that comes from within the self and cannot be given by anyone or anything else. What's so joyful about that? It means that you need not depend on anything outside of yourself anymore to enjoy real security. It becomes manifest in the world of self-validation, which is an experience of life where you feel great because you *are* great and not because someone told you so. Life with self-validation offers freedom, whereas when we chase security (as the world refers to security), we never leave the zone of insecurity. In attempting to create certainty, we never actually shake uncertainty. We make security and certainty goals our destinations.

Uncertainty as a Gift

What can uncertainty offer you? To have that space where the unknown, the unexpected, and the surprising emerges is to have the opportunity for new and great things to happen; to be able to trust that what emerges will be right for you brings with it reason not to worry; to live with confidence in knowing that the potential of the unknown will, in fact, serve you so much better than the slavery of the known, is a gift so rich that it will ensure your freedom forever. This unfamiliar territory is filled with the riches of potentiality. Embracing uncertainty is about re-framing life; it is looking with different eyes at the same facts, and discovering if they produce a different answer, or even a new set of questions.

What would it be like for you to open yourself to wherever you are; to realize that this is the perfect place to be right now; to trust yourself; to trust the universe, and embrace who and where you are right now? All very fine you might say, but if I'm out of a job and waiting in line to get my social welfare, what's so perfect about that?

Life's situations only have the meaning that we give them. For the person who is upset because they are unemployed and collecting social assistance, life offers no less opportunity for choice or decision than it did when they were employed. What he or she does with that moment in relation to their choices, will be influenced by the meaning of that moment, which is the meaning that they alone give it. No one or nothing else is responsible, or to blame.

Relating to Uncertainty
For the contradiction of uncertainty to be of service to us, we need to work towards uncertainty as being a gift, an opportunity, a gateway, a place of potentiality. Most of us see uncertainty as a place of fear and insecurity – a place to be avoided.

It is always our choice to see uncertainty as a gift, as a moment of potentiality. Then uncertainty is utterly transformed into a powerful and priceless gift. It becomes a force of creation. At times it will be a real struggle to allow yourself to see the gift, grasp the opportunity, and embrace the potentiality. You may be overcome with the fear that can exist in uncertainty, but that is not a reason to give up. It is, in fact, the perfect reason to go further into trusting and allowing the uncertainty to become your most abundant provider of all you need.

Our society sees uncertainty as undesirable, and we are expected to be compliant with this view of the world and play society's game of certainty, which is the tyranny of what I term 'controlled certainty'.

This controlled certainty is all about binding you to a life of constant payments and the recurring fear of not meeting obligations. It limits the freedom of self-expression, so that you can have the certainty of a job in order to give you the home and the lifestyle you are encouraged to want. But what if you are unhappy or uneasy with the way your life is unfolding? What if this certainty is not providing the well-being, the peace, and the joy of life for you? Do you have to struggle through it, because you know that change that is too radical would put you outside the comfort zone of certainty; put you outside what others accept or what society demands? How is controlled certainty working for you?

Being Fair to Uncertainty

What if there is something fundamental missing? What can you do? This contradiction is about you asking if your life is serving you well. Are you getting from your life what you want, and what you need? If the answer is 'no', how do you address the implications of this?

Understanding Uncertainty

Understanding healthy uncertainty is a launching pad to a new place within the self and a new place within the world. It is one of the secret ingredients of having life play out the way you want and dream; it is one of the more direct routes available to peace and it is the road of least resistance. This requires a decision to take the necessary steps so that uncertainty can unveil for you, your true potentiality. In good contradiction tradition, you will probably not like the initial feelings that accompany the embracing of uncertainty.

All the clichéd understandings of uncertainty will be hard to dispel. You may feel insecure, unsure, and ill equipped, but working through these feelings with the vision and commitment necessary, will allow you to not only survive the unsettling early stages of this contradiction, but truly thrive with the revelations that await you. All of this occurs as you allow uncertainty to work its own particular magic on you. It will be through embracing the uncertainty, that deep peace of mind will be discovered; when you realize that you do not need the external 'certainties' to put you at ease. It is in this uncertain space that you will be able to acknowledge that this is where you are and you already have all you need.

You will be out of your comfort zone according to society's standards, but you are in a zone where you are in control by allowing the unknown to be your teacher. There is no promise of comfort during the transition, but there is a promise that the new will bring you closer to your dream. You will be faced with the fear of the endless possibilities, but it is good to also allow yourself to get excited by those possibilities and make that excitement your focus.

Change is a Part of the Package
Entering the world of contradiction is critical to entering the world of change. Change is essential if we are to allow

uncertainty to teach us, empower us, and release us; change, not for the sake of change, but change that occurs as a result of your journey to turn the discovery of your potential into reality in your daily life. We spend so much of our lives trying to avoid change, but it is inevitable. Change is happening all the time. All the things that exist outside of you are potentially things that you can lose in life. If you depend upon them to make you feel better, stronger or more successful, you are in for a big surprise when they disappear. This loneliness is more painful than any physical pain you could experience. To wake and discover that you have lost what was most important to you, and that you are a stranger to yourself, is a moment when all internal systems begin to grind to a halt. This is a spiritual pain, an aching that comes from deep within, and it screams at you to take notice. Thus, you begin the healing process so that you can realign life and its purpose.

For many people who have had years of conditioning in external validation, there is a chance that the pain of losing the source of validation will be so significant that it effectively finishes them off to a certain extent. They no longer have the strength, stamina, or the capacity to rebuild, and to begin looking within. We can get so stuck in the different stages of grieving the loss that getting through the process bleeds us of the little energy that is left.

Achieving a personal connection with the true self is too valuable to say no to, simply because you are afraid of change. Change is going to happen anyway, so it's better that you work with change, and become a lover of the self, so you do not lose the self when the big moments in life happen, and things change.

When you are learning to be at peace with uncertainty the prospect of change will not frighten you, it will invigorate you. It is when you are stuck in the swamp of needing to be certain, that you become afraid of change because it threatens your control and takes you out of your comfort zone. Life will do what life does, and it will not stop to ask if you are okay, or if you are ready for the change. It will happen with little notice, and often without providing a safety net to catch you. Your life is the result of your creating, nothing else. How you deal with the changes and shifts in life, will create the experiences that shape your future. It is wise to know who you are and why you are.

Change can be beautiful and powerful, or ugly and destructive. The victim will fall in times of change, but the strong will grow and transform. There are a number of elements of life that need to be embraced to live in and with uncertainty.

Engaging In 'the process' of moving forward and living with uncertainty.
There are only a few tools you need in your tool box to begin experiencing the certainty of uncertainty. Once you are familiar with the four tools for living in uncertainty, put tomorrow aside as a day to test the experience and see what happens.

1. *Courage*

It takes courage to face the challenge of wandering into the unknown. Sometimes it can be difficult to move from where you are, even if it is filled with a certain level of pain and discomfort, because you are at least familiar with that reality. You know that even though it has brought you some challenges, you have managed to keep going and survive thus far. Part of the illusion of the pain you are feeling in moving into the unknown, is the fear of failure; what if the pain ahead is too much? What if I cannot manage it? What if it finishes me off altogether? What if the change creates more discomfort? What if I lose friends because of the change?

It is also important to know that most of the time in life, we do not fear failure as much as we fear success. Something deep within us is always whispering 'don't do it', 'it won't work', and these voices can be powerful in terms of keeping you stuck. As you hear these voices, know also that there is a voice within saying you can.

2. *Trust*

There are no guarantees that you will experience the life you dream of, even if you take the steps toward that success. Remember that the journey is what matters most, not the destination. It is important to bring trust with you on your journey. This is not an invitation to trust an outside force, person, God or situation (I have no doubt that there is an external power at play, but I believe it is only accessed through an authentic and internal connection to self). This is an invitation to trust that you have the resources within you to find a way through the new situations; the courage to accept your flaws and failings; the confidence to stop blaming, judging and pointing the finger; the heart to celebrate your new way; the emotion to feel the love you are seeking, and the assurance that the detail is only detail. Know that you will manage it in order to make the journey enjoyable. This trust is what you need when you wake up in the midst of not knowing where you are, how you got here, or where you are going to end up.

3. *Know that you are more thany our feelings*
We all get swamped with many feelings as we go through life, and as we take on the challenge of change. We often identify with these feelings and, at some level, we begin to feel that we ARE the feeling. However, feelings are only feelings. It is true that they have power in our lives and can cause an effect that is difficult to put into words.

However, you are not just your feelings; you are much greater than your emotions. Emotions happen as a result of a choice you have made. We get to choose how we wish to react to a given situation or circumstance in a given way. Your feelings are attached to the meaning you give these situations or circumstances. They are the physical manifestations of your thoughts and beliefs in that moment. Feelings are your friends; both the 'good' and the 'bad' are there to serve you in terms of attaining your higher good. In truth, feelings are neither good nor bad, they are simply feelings, but they hold something invaluable for you to learn from. Every feeling has a message to bring to you.

There is a simple way to deal with this dilemma. If a feeling, thought, focus, perception or understanding is making you feel great about yourself and supports your confidence and self-esteem, it is worth holding onto and building upon. If the feeling, thought, focus, perception or understanding is creating a reality of negativity, poverty consciousness, depression, lack/not enough, it is telling you something has to change. Remember, you have the power to choose a different reality, a different thought, focus, understanding or perception. You are the creator and the author. What you get in life is the result of how you live life and contribute to the needs of the authentic you.

4. *Allowing failure*

So often we use our achievements in life to place a value on who we are and what we have to offer. We observe our behaviors, our job titles, our families, our wealth and our relationships, and based on what we see, we draw conclusions. We label ourselves as successful or, if we don't see what is there as successful, then we can label ourselves as failing, having failed or a failure. However, all of these judgements about being successful or a failure, are built on the illusion of what the world says is success or not. The task here is to allow everything to be just what it is and try to change nothing, instead begin to see everything as a messenger that brings with it a powerful teaching. Look for that teaching and know it is there.

The word 'failure' is such a powerful word and has so many direct line connections to other words that hold us in a pattern of the negative. Think failure and you may think: not good enough, less than, not enough, lacking, poor, shamed, embarrassed, guilty, underachieving, broken, fallen, lower, negative, struggle, poor me, powerless, and the list goes on. Our world has taught us that failure is not a road you want to travel, and yet the reality of life is one that says failure cannot be avoided. Think about this for a moment and you may get an insight into why so many people are negative throughout their lives. Can you see the confusion and the patterns of thought that can come from this incongruence?

Living in uncertainty does mean that you live in a place where you are without knowledge. To truly embrace uncertainty means that you have the most valuable knowledge of all, the knowledge of wisdom: you are assured of what is in any given moment, you are assured that the moment is the result of your choices, and you have the confidence to know that what is to be will be born from the choices that you make in that place and at that time. From this space there is nothing to fear, there is no possibility of getting caught up in the right or wrong of society's ways, and there is nothing that can take you by surprise. Uncertainty allows for the unexpected, it invites the unexpected, it celebrates the unexpected, and it creates an opportunity for the unexpected to hold within it the key you have been searching for, to unlock the code to your potentiality.

Contradiction # 2

The Only Way Out
Is Through It

Dealing with the pain in our life

We are meant to know freedom, peace and joy. It is possible to move through our current challenges and circumstances with so much power and intention that we no longer feel the emotional pain life can bring. There is a way out, but it is only by going 'through' the pain that we get out of the pain. There is no other option, other than avoidance, and even that is not possible. This is because what we resist and avoid in life tends to keep coming back seeking its completion. We all have feelings, both positive and negative, whether they are acknowledged or not. Emotional pain is a result of any one of those (pesky) negative feelings.

In recognizing that there is something we want 'out of,' we must first acknowledge that we are in it. Once we have allowed this realization, we have taken the first step in passing through it and finding the way out. This holds true in all of life's situations, but the true power of this statement is experienced when it is understood in the context of the emotional pain we endure in life, and the seemingly endless patterns of stagnation. All too often, we think we are fighting the internal turmoil, when in fact we are searching for the solutions. The search is a necessary part of the solution, and therefore, so too is the pain that comes with the search; they go hand in hand. Being in emotional pain does not mean that you are not close to a solution. It can even be an indicator that the solution is closer than you think.

When we believe that we are in a battle with some aspect of our internal or external life, we become distracted from focusing on or experiencing peace. This state of mind seldom frees us from the pain we are feeling. Instead, it simply distracts us from the real issue, and holds us in a reinforced position of powerlessness.

We cannot expect that a distraction of any type will make hurt go away for any more than a brief moment. Nor can we expect that looking in a different direction will make that which we are not looking at, disappear. Living as if something does not exist will not give us an experience of life. What is there is there; where we are is where we are; and what is happening is indeed, happening. Avoidance of life's situations simply means that we will be faced with it again at another time. Until that time comes, we will live with an invisible shadow hanging over, and in some cases haunting us.

When emotional pain finds its way into our world, there is only one way to ensure that it is temporary, and that it does not last any longer than necessary. We must recognize the pain and give it its rightful title; meaning name it. Accept the fact that it will not go away until it has been processed, and that we have come to a full understanding of what it is really about. Learn the true nature of the hurt, in terms of what it is bringing, and embrace the journey that the healing is demanding.

Understanding, healing, and peace happen out of experiencing life and all that comes with it. They are not achieved simply by reading a book of logic or by engaging in a program of positive thinking. 'Experiencing the feeling' in detail, means that we go deeper into it. Only by fully experiencing these feelings, will we find what we need to heal them, and only by going through each hurt, can we get out of it permanently.

Consider doing these action steps to help 'you' acknowledge what you are feeling, and to assist you in working through it:
--Focus on something other than the negative. Try to replace the negative thought with a positive thought.
--Put the mind's attention on an opposite reality. Remember that the 'Law of Attraction' is at play in our lives, and we draw to us that which we think about.
--Engage in behavior that is more representative of what is wanted, rather than what we do not want. This would also be considered as taking action toward our desired goal.

Lifting the Illusion
There is a powerful illusion that we seem to live with; the illusion that the emotional pain we are going through is bad and to be avoided. This could not be farther from the truth. Painful thoughts or feelings are neither bad, nor to be avoided. They are simply something that we experience and they are no different

than joy, peace or happiness. For some reason, we have a world filled with teachings of how to create a positive state of mind, as well as how to create a quick fix for all of the things that are not positive. The negative issues in our lives are not bad in and of them selves, but are in fact, a healthy part of the process that is life. However, they are only a part of the process. If we allow ourselves to believe that this is all we require, we are working with an incomplete map. Therefore, the healing we seek will continue to seem distant and unknown.

The problem we often experience in life is the idea that things need to be good or bad, positive or negative, right or wrong. To have an experience of true peace, fulfillment, joy, or success, there is a need to move beyond judgment and the tendency to label things. As long as we are putting labels on people or situations, we are boxing them into categories that prevent a more authentic and honest experience from happening. This same illusion tells us that pain is not good, and as a result of this, we try to find the things in life that we are told are good. We are constantly seeking something that is outside of us, and in doing so we are not dealing with the reality of what is within us. This is simply avoidance, and it is inspired by ignorance; by not knowing the true value of the experience we call pain and suffering.

Therefore, emotional pain is not a bad thing. We are simply having 'an experience'. If we allow ourselves to understand the experience, we will discover many hidden gifts that will allow us to create a different outcome than what might normally be expected. That is not to say that what we are going through is easy. There is no doubt that there is a good case to show that it is, in fact, very difficult. However, if we perceive what is happening as bad, we will be making a significant contribution to continuing the suffering we are going through. Considering this, we always need to be very careful for it is true that perception creates reality. It is possible for us to get to a place where we are living with it and healing, but not suffering.

Another illusion we often harbor is that we are processing it when we are talking about it, sharing it, crying about it, figuring it out, and attempting to apply logic to it. However, this is not necessarily so. These are simply things we do when we need to blow off steam, and reduce the pressure of all that is boiling up inside of us. To heal the pain and move through it so that it no longer haunts us, we need to engage the highest level of the process that few books teach, few schools include in their curriculum, and very few people know about, let alone know how to process.

Why We Avoid Our Pain
There are many reasons: It hurts, we are afraid of it, we believe that focusing on it will only hurt more, we don't know how to deal with it, we know that there is something attached to the feeling that we simply want to remain in denial of, and the list goes on. However, avoiding it only ensures that it will be around a lot longer. If we truly want to live without any kind of pain in our lives, avoidance is not a solution. It is only a defense

mechanism, and a sure way to attract and receive more of the same.

You will know you are avoiding the source of the turmoil when it, or the situation that caused it, continues to hurt you, continues to cause you to react, or continues to bring conflict within yourself or others. Many of us live for years, decades or in some cases, throughout our entire life with unresolved pain.

The Importance of 'Going Through the Pain

It may be difficult to accept this when you are in the middle of a life crisis, but the simple fact of the matter is that pain does not exist, it is an illusion, a compelling illusion; but an illusion, nonetheless. It is for this reason that you are required (by self), to go into the pain. Imagine what your life would look and feel like if you were to discover the truth: that pain does not really exist and is nothing other than a created state of being. It is a result of how you think, and what you choose to believe. By allowing yourself to go into the pain you are confronting all the things that are causing you distress and discomfort. Once there, it is possible for you to understand the true nature of the pain. By understanding the true nature of anything, you have the tools required to change the experience.

Let's use an example of physical pain: You are living with a toothache and the pain of the ache is so much that you are not sleeping well, you are not eating properly, and you are continually experiencing mood swings. The pain is severe and you know that the only way out is to go to the dentist. It is true that the experience of the root canal can be painful. For some, the pain of the visit to the dentist can far exceed the pain of the toothache. However, in order for you to regulate your sleep, eating habits, and balance your mood swings, it is 'essential' that you go through the pain of the root canal. In truth, you are allowing yourself to experience the full extent of the toothache in order to have it resolved. 'You are going through pain to get out of pain'.

Once you have gone through the dental visit and had the toothache addressed, you are on the road to recovery and before you know it, the pain is a distant memory. Avoiding the toothache, or continually medicating so you don't feel the pain, simply means that you are putting off today what you will eventually have to deal with. Either that, or you will become so good at avoiding the pain by never dealing with it (not to mention the suffering entailed), that you will simply spread the problem throughout all of your teeth in time. Your problems will then grow to an unmanageable level, one that culminates in a lot more pain in the long run. So it is with ALL pain, especially the emotional and psychological traumas of life.

Seven Insights into the World of Pain

1. *Pain needs to be addressed and will be addressed. No matter how much we avoid our issues, they will turn up in our life, asking for and demanding attention.*
   The only way out is through. When there is pain, there can be little else. In order to live without it, we need to learn to

know and understand it, discover its origins, and hear its call. We must become aware of what it is telling us that is needed for the healing to happen. On the path of healing, we are required to become a warrior, and we are asked to take our place on the battlefield of our own inner struggles. There is nowhere else to be, other than in the midst of our own everything. What else is there?

Healing (i.e. going through it) is the process of processing fact from fiction. There is little to do other than to be in the emotional moment and be very aware. See, feel, and hear what is there, and above all, honor it. Name it for what it really is and allow it to be so you do not miss anything. That is what 'going through it' really means. Become one with it. There is little point in trying to ignore, avoid or run away from life's emotional trauma and dramas. This is called acceptance. It lives within you and until you finally surrender to that fact and face it, it will remain within you for an eternity.

Think of a children's mythological story and imagine the hero of the story facing the dragon. You know there is going to be a battle. The hero knows there is no point in hiding, no point in running, no point in ignoring, and no point in denying. He knows that the time is now and it is better to die in the name of freedom, than to have a long slow death, hiding in the crevices and the caves of avoidance.

As you can see, we need not be afraid of emotional pain. If you are not dealing with it, diving into the midst of it and facing it, it is foolish to think that you can escape its grip, resist suffering at its hands, and/or live with its consequences. You will be missing out on life by refusing to face it. This can cost you your dreams; even cause you to stop dreaming. Facing it would be the warrior's way. Remember, nothing is as it seems.

2. *Emotional pain is an illusion. In reality, it is simply an experience.*
Unfortunately, most of us have learned by conditioning, to identify it as something that is negative and bad. You can, however, develop understanding.

Since we have been conditioned and coded to believe that emotional pain is a bad experience, we tend to switch on all the self-protection buttons, as soon as we get wind of it showing up in our lives. These defense mechanisms are an effort to cut off the feelings and dislocate the thinking (or the awareness of what we are really thinking). However, in cutting off the 'pain' we are cutting off the experience. In cutting off the experience, we are cutting off the learning. By cutting off the learning, we are cutting off the growth, and in cutting off growth, we are choosing to stay exactly where we are (emotionally, psychologically and physically). I guess we could rephrase that from 'choosing to stay exactly where we are', to 'choosing not to create a new version of who we are'.

We are always growing or shrinking; getting strong or getting weak; becoming awake or falling deeper into sleep.

The experience we call 'painful' is simply an experience. It is a feeling that is important to experience in full. This does not mean that we need to feel it forever, it simply means that there must be a period of time when the pain is felt at the fullest level. This is a part of the process of getting through it, and ultimately out of it. All of our feelings, experiences, and situations are teachers. Why would you discriminate against one just because you say you don't like it, or it feels bad? Perhaps it is because we have been conditioned to believe that painful feelings are bad. Therefore, we spend the rest of our lives in avoidance.

There is no way to know what pain is emotionally and psychologically about, or what it has to offer until we experience it intimately. In this way, we become aware that it holds many blessings. It is no different than any other experience of life. It can bring us great lessons and great wisdom if we choose to see it in such a way. Of course, because we all have free will, we always have the choice to move through it or remain in resistance. Resistance is an exhausting and difficult position to take.

3. *The experience called 'pain' is one of the greatest gifts you could ever have in your life. However, what makes it a gift is what happens as you move through it and how you use it.*

Let's say that you feel stuck in a moment of darkness. The pain is so bad that you sometimes feel you will never get past it. Now imagine that this darkness is the shadow side of your life. We know that for there to be a shadow there must also be a light. Both realities are simply aspects of you. Knowing that the darkness can run deep, it is fair to suggest that you can believe there is an equally deep light in your life. To phrase it differently, you are also a deep light. All you need to do is go on the journey of discovering the part of YOU that is light.

If you follow your pain and learn how to track it, it will lead you to a portal into a part of yourself that you may never have known existed. When allowed to teach you, your emotional pain will bring you to places, show you things, and educate you about who you really are. This will be well beyond anything that this world will or ever could have introduced you to. It will open doorways and gateways, and will drive you to the deepest and furthest points of the universe that exist within you. From this experience you will find out that all that really matters is the silence, compassion, purpose, meaning, understanding, joy, bliss, and most important of all, peace and love.

It is important to note here that simply feeling the pain is not enough. You must follow the feeling to see where it brings you. All that is asked is that you continue to follow the feelings as they surface. Switch off the mind in terms of judgement and become the one that observes what you experience. It is then that you are in the hands of the master and you will learn the way of the warrior.

4. ***The consequence of pain can be heaven or hell on earth, and your choices will determine which you live in.***
    Because we have free will, we can live in and from the feeling, or we can live in and from a different perspective. It is not unusual for people to be influenced by their pain, yet not even be aware of it. Nonetheless, they are living in a place of deficit or negative focus and for that, they are paying a significant price, namely, peace.

Only yesterday I was walking down the promenade of a beautifully quaint fishing village in the Portuguese Algarve with my wife. We stopped to chat for a moment with someone we knew. Within only a few minutes we learned that this woman can't sit in the sun, as it has an 'awful' effect on her. She 'suffered' that day with the 'incredible' humidity, and was 'really lonely' being there on her own. She was finding it 'beyond difficult' and couldn't walk on the beach as she had 'injured' her ankle while walking another day... and the list of woes continued. Here is a woman who is living out of her pain body. Somewhere within this woman is pain, both emotional and physical. She seems to experience everything in life through the lens of that pain. There is an unresolved pain, an old hurt, a significant untended wound, or a feeling of being unable to belong. I don't think it's important to try to guess what it is, but it's obvious that she is in pain and it is affecting her life. Like everyone, she can make a choice to change perspective and enter a process of dealing with the cause. She will realize that she can sit in the sun, the humidity isn't so bad, and her ankle doesn't hurt so much anymore. More than that, she will begin to love her own company and loneliness will become a thing of the past.

5. *If you are still feeling and living in pain, you are not plugging into the bigger picture.*
    Challenges will always be a part of our lives in one form or another, but only you can decide whether it brings you down or adds to your life experience as a positive and great teacher.

Of course, there IS a bigger picture. You do have a purpose; there is meaning. The whole essence of life is a fantastic tapestry filled with magic and miracles waiting for you to discover and then activate them. (Now don't go looking outside of yourself for this magic and these miracles, they are not there. You are both the magic and the miracles. In order to activate them, you must activate yourself). Once you know about this bigger picture and experience it, your life changes. You stop living from the negative prospective of pain. You begin to live a different experience and to appreciate the experience of the great 'teacher' that pain is. You can no longer remain the same as you were, before plugging into the wisdom of life.

When you catch yourself moaning, complaining, responding in a negative context to your hurt, blaming, judging, suffering or acting up, you can choose to remind yourself that you have the blinkers on. Focus on knowing that there is a bigger picture, and that everything in life is not quite as it seems. Next, simply begin and continue to follow the feelings. After that, you need do very little. It will all happen within you so that you will be free to observe and learn.

6. *Life is not what it seems; you are not what you seem.*
Go in search of what this means. Here's a hint: trust your heart. Do nothing about it just now, wait until you have finished reading all the chapters and come back to reflect on what this means.

7. *Dealing with pain means dealing with love.*
When you are avoiding the inner turmoil, you are avoiding spending time with love; yes, love. Your pain needs compassion, understanding, acceptance, forgiveness, healing and peace – all the ingredients and elements of love. Maybe the real issue is being compassionate with yourself; being gentle, listening, allowing, holding the fear and the loss without trying to fix it. Perhaps you have been in denial and there is an issue with understanding and accepting that pain is even there and that you are hurt. It is possible that you have been building up a psychological barrier so strong that you are convinced you are strong when in fact, there is a part of you that is truly broken and needs to scream, cry, own, honor and feel it. Is it that you don't know how to forgive? Maybe you are trying to forgive someone else, but it is not working. The answer is: Stop trying. You can only forgive yourself, you cannot forgive anyone else. Perhaps you don't know how

to forgive yourself or what you need to forgive yourself for. Do you even know what 'healing' is? Or is that just a word that makes sense from what you have been told about it, and that makes you want it? What about peace? and what about compassion? If you allow compassion in, there is no need for forgiveness at all.

Recognizing unresolved issues

You will see very clear signs of unresolved issues if you allow yourself to step back and look at your life in the context of how you think, act, feel, and experience life.

Seeing unresolved pain in how you think

When you catch yourself being any of the following, it is time to stop and take stock of the situation. Make a conscious effort to change your behavior. Being:

--cynical	--worried
--critical	--short-tempered
--judgemental	--negative
--upset	--afraid
--always finding fault with the world, events, or people around you	

Here you are seeing the effects of the issues that are alive and well within you. This can be the result of something that seems very significant or something that you would judge as insignificant, but nonetheless, it is there. You are living according to its demands whenever you see any of these characteristics show up in your life.

Seeing unresolved pain in how you act

Do the same when you become aware of any of these behaviors:
--shouting at someone
--laughing at someone
--speaking negatively about yourself or another person
--trying to make yourself look good by making someone else look bad
--stealing
--damaging another's possessions
--threatening someone
--physically hurting someone
--not supporting those around you who need help

At these times, you are seeing the consequences of pain within you that has become your master in those moments. You may not even be aware that any of these things are a part of your life, but the truth is that you don't need to know you are in pain to be in pain.

Seeing unresolved pain in how you feel. This is when you feel:

--sad
--depressed
--angry humiliated
--flooded with emotion
--not good enough
--not smart enough

--enraged
--shamed
--humiliated
--guilty
--out of control
--fearful

--or seeing your unresolved pain taking over and ruling your life.

Seeing unresolved pain in how you experience life:

--when the world around you seems to be against you
--when you can't find support
--when you are lonely
--when nothing works out for you
--when you continually fail at things
--when you see only what is wrong with someone or something
--when you are continually worried about money
--when relationships are always rocky
--when you can't seem to find your purpose and meaning in this life, you are witnessing your own pain, and the pain that is breathing and fighting to stay alive within you.

There is nothing to fear, you're already there
No matter what excuse you use for avoiding any of the above issues, you are only fooling yourself. The very fact that you are avoiding it tells you that you are in it, feeling it, and experiencing it. Avoiding it is NOT working. The idea of avoiding it is simply something you tell yourself in order to try to believe that you are fine and all is okay. However, the simple fact of the matter is that when you are in it, you are in it, and the only way out is to go through it.

Let's say that you have something in your life that hurts: a past relationship, a childhood abuse, a fear of some kind, an insecurity of some sort, a feeling that things will fail or a belief that you will be judged if you follow your dreams. Suppose that you avoid the pain most of the time, but every so often it surfaces and causes you distress. On a scale of one to ten, you say that the pain represents a six when it comes up and a four the rest of the time.

46

This is due to the fact that you don't always feel it as much, but it is always lurking there in the shadows of your day. You are now spending your life in a pain level of somewhere between four and six. You know that it will never get any better as you are not doing anything to heal it. Something inside you is telling you not to deal with it because it hurts. If you were to really focus on it, you would find it may hurt even more. At the same time something else inside of you is telling you to deal with it once and for all and get passed it. You know it is the only way you can move on with your life, but the fear of the pain in dealing with it is always enough to keep you from going there.

Now let's say that you decide to deal with it. In dealing with it, the focus that you bring to it creates a pain level of nine on the scale. During the healing process, the pain level slowly reduces from a nine to an eight, from an eight to a seven, from a seven to a six and so on. Within a certain period of time, the pain level will reduce to the point of no longer registering as pain.

The Choices Available:
1. Live with a significant pain level of between four and six for the rest of your life.
2. Allow a pain level of nine for a short while, that continually reduces and eventually eliminates the pain from your life forever.

It is that simple. The fact of the matter is that because you are already having the experience of the pain, you do not need to be afraid of it. Why be afraid of that which you are already experiencing? Is it not better to face it and heal it, than to spend your life being a servant to it?

Engaging In 'the process' of moving through it and healing our life

There is a process that we can engage in that will allow us to heal our life to the point of knowing peace. This process will bring us to a place of resolution in such a way that our pain will be healed permanently. We will also discover that once we begin the process, and by focusing on one hurtful situation at a time, we will be healing aspects of all our negative issues. It is likely that we will find within this process an equation that stands true in relation to each issue we can identify. Once we have actually applied this system to healing one area of our life, we will have the knowledge and experience to deal with all of our issues. Most of what we thought were 'individual' issues, will show themselves to be expressions of other areas that need our attention.

'The Process'

This will require you to be 100% honest with yourself. Anything else will simply facilitate your continual avoidance of dealing with things and be detrimental to the point of healing.

The following steps can take up to an hour to complete for each painful issue you want to bring healing to. You may need to revisit the same issue a number of times over a few weeks to really know that you have allowed the healing to happen.

1. Accept the fact that there IS hurt to be healed.
2. Accept the fact that something different needs to happen in order for the situation to be healed.
3. Give it a name. Do not try to cover it with a nice cheery, pink cloud, red ribbon, positive title. Simply call it as it is, and allow yourself to be 'in the moment' of acknowledging it for what it is. Take some time in a quiet space where you will not be disturbed. As you sit in a relaxed position (not lying down), with your eyes closed, focus your mind on the pain. Imagine the pain getting bigger within you, amplify it as much as is possible. Really allow yourself to feel what is going on inside you. If you get emotional, allow the emotion to express itself gently and kindly. Do not hold back the tears. They are healthy and soul-cleansing.
4. Become aware of the feeling and talk out loud to yourself about what you are experiencing:

>--Where in your body do you feel pain? Is it only emotional, or has it manifested into the physical? Tune into it as much as you can and amplify it even more.

>--What does it feel like? Describe it as much as you can. As you go through this experience do not judge what is happening or try to make sense of it (healing happens in a place where sense and logic rarely go). Simply watch with your imagination what is happening and talk as much as you can to yourself as the experience unfolds.

>--What thoughts come up as you are tuning into the feeling? Hold onto the memory of the thoughts and

follow each thought for a moment and see where it brings you. It may bring you to another thought, or a word, a memory, a new feeling, a color, a sense of something or someone. Simply allow yourself to follow what is happening and do not try to direct it, allow it to guide you.

--Trust what is coming up and do not question it. At a logical level some of what happens may not make sense to you; that's ok, remember this is about healing. It is not about making sense, being right, or having everything sorted into perfect order.

--As you observe the thoughts and the images that appear, imagine that they are all moving towards your heart.

--Tune into the most dominant feeling that you are experiencing.

--Imagine that feeling moving towards your heart and allow the feeling to move completely into the center of your heart.

--Become aware of the feeling of your body being healed, as you focus on your heart space. Do not wait to feel something, just allow yourself to know that the healing is happening. The feeling will follow in many cases.

--Remain in that position and allow that to happen until the healing is complete. You will know when that happens as you will experience a significant shift in how you feel.

--Next, take a moment of silence again and go back to the heart space. Ask your heart to tell you what needs to change in your life and what you need to do in order for the healing to be fully integrated.

--Finally, open your eyes and immediately begin to write down the entire experience you just had. Write down all the details of what you saw, heard, felt and experienced.

The only way out is through it, but once you allow yourself to BE in your pain, the hardest part is done.

Don't confuse knowing with being in your pain.

There is a significant difference between having an awareness and a mindful understanding of what our painful situations are. Being 'in' our pain means sitting in a space where we allow it to surface and become as big and strong as its needs to become. We feel it throughout our body. We are not judging it, trying to make it go away, controlling it, attaching logic to it, denying it, minimizing it, telling ourselves it's not that bad, or finding a distraction to allow us avoid it. These are all things we do every day because we get busy, but they do not allow for healing. Instead they simply feed the pain and ensure that it will hang around a little longer.

Moving through the healing process will leave you somewhat vulnerable. Therefore, be sure to be gentle with yourself. Be careful to avoid all negative people and environments, for at least a week after you go through the healing process. In fact, you might want to do that permanently.

Contradiction # 3

Courage Comes After You Do It, Not Before

When listening to the stories of how people changed their lives and took the unthinkable leap into a new world, it is not unusual to hear them talk about not understanding how they managed to do it. Many will say 'I just did it, I had no choice, and something had to change'. You may even hear them talk about how they realized that any pain associated with change, no matter how difficult, couldn't be any greater than the pain of leaving things the way they were.

It takes courage to jump from an old life into a new life, and seldom will you meet someone who had the courage the first time they made the leap. What was it that finally caused them to flick the switch and throw caution to the wind? For some, it was the desperation of how they were feeling in the old life; for some it was simply a knowing that if they did not do it they would live in regret; and for others it was the decision to awaken, and know that anything that offers the potential for something new, is better than something that creates only pain and stagnation.

Perhaps the next time they make a move, create a change or totally uproot their life, they will do it with courage. This is only because they have done it once before and survived. They now know that everything will be okay, and that makes the jumping easier.

When the first leap happens, there is often not an ounce of courage to be seen, rather whirlwinds of fear, anxiety, stress, panic, and a sense of surrender. Those who have made the change and created a new lease on life, can also remember that the change took longer than they expected, because they were waiting to find the courage. They thought that courage would be there to support them as they made their leap. Courage is the bravery to do what has to be done with a knowing that regardless of the outcome, everything will be okay. Courage is the nerve, the pluck, and the daring needed to go where you have never gone before, and to do it with an assurance that this is the right thing for you. How can anyone take their first real leap in life with a knowing, a confidence or an assurance, if they have never done it before and know that everything will be okay?

Waiting for courage
There are two sides to this coin. Waiting for the blast of courage to take action can be a time of excitement and hope. We can often imagine the results of the action we will take, as soon as that courage kicks in. We can imagine the change it will bring to our life, and we can even see in our mind's eye the person we will become.

The waiting is often justified by a logic telling us that when a certain something happens, or a certain number of things happen, we will have in place all we need to take the plunge. There is a belief that having control of certain things, and having all our 'ducks lined up in a row', in the order we think we need them, will be the perfect time to take action. To an extent there is some truth in this. There are certain things in life that we need, and want to have lined up and sorted out. We do this in order for our dreams to get all of our attention.

However, there are certain things in life that will never be lined up, that will never be ready, and that will never be sorted out in the way needed for us to have the courage to move forward. These things vary depending on the individual, and depending on the dream. It is not possible to say what they are for you (only you can do that). Take the time to go within, and you will soon learn what it is that you need to stop trying to get ready or organized; all that is required is action.

There will always be something that cannot be controlled, organized or managed and until we learn that, we will be stuck in the waiting room of life, as the world moves on around us. It can be a painful room to get stuck in, while the windows to the rest of the world are often big and very clear. We can see all of the people, opportunities, possibilities, days, months and years, relationships, potential wins, and new insights flying by. We find ourselves in someone else's world, as we sit there quietly waiting for the doctor of life to call us in, and write us a prescription so we can collect our courage at the *'lifearmacy'*. Well, it is never going to happen, because that call will never come. There is no prescription waiting to bring us the courage we need and want so badly.

'The courage we seek to take action only comes to us once we have taken action.'

Taking Action

Taking the leap means making a decision to take action, and then taking the action, whatever that might be. There is no point in planning, dreaming, visioning and creating an image of the future we want, without taking the leap. We will only find the courage to do what scares us most -- by doing it.

Most of the time we will not be ready for it, nor will we be sure of what is going to happen when we take the leap. There is always the risk that it will end up very differently than what we imagined, hoped or envisioned.

Don't let it stop you from taking the leap. You create your reality; you are the only one that can map out your reality and your future, and only you can make it work out, or cause it to fail. Only you can take the leap, and if you depend on another to take the leap with you, you will discover that once you are over the edge, you are on your own anyway. It is a massive step, unless it's not, but that will depend on you and how you choose to perceive the experience. The only thing that will guide you towards a thinking of one or the other, will be your understanding of reality. Remember that choosing to stay in the same place, doing the same thing, and having the same experience will have a significant set of consequences attached. Regardless of what your decision is, you are creating your future. It is better to die trying than live dreaming.

Be a Silent Observer

As you take the actions needed to create your future, it is most important to live in the present moment. Many people ask, 'How can you live in the moment when you are off planning for the future, or dealing with a mess from the past?' The answer is simple; you look to the future only to create your vision of what lies ahead. You measure that future reality with nothing other than the way you are feeling right now with your emotions, your mindset, and your beliefs. As soon as you can see and feel this future image or picture, you let go of it, and become 100% present in the moment you are in. If your future vision is 'good' and healthy, then get busy being the best you can be, to ensure that future becomes a reality.

However, if the future you looked into is not what you would like to experience, then you must get totally present in this moment and live in a way that will create a different future experience. Don't spend your time worrying about the future or you will create precisely the future you have worried about. You will create the future as a mirror reflection of this moment if you so choose. You will relive the present in regards to your emotions, attention, beliefs, motivations, focus, worries, and even your frustrations, unless you change your present way of living and your vision for the future.

When we speak of a silent observer, we are really talking about becoming an observer of our entire life experience at a whole new level. We become an observer of our past, our present and our future for the purpose of watching, learning, interacting and evolving. This observation involves our imagination, our memories and our emotions.

We become an observer of our own actions in life and the relationships in which we engage. We become aware of how we act, the intention behind the actions, the details of the actions themselves, and the consequences of the actions. With relationships, we observe ourself in the relationship and how we relate to it.

Is it the drama or the joy that you are working from? What are the consequences of the interaction, and the experience of the moment you are observing? In living as the silent observer, you get an aerial view of your reality, and this learning opportunity allows you to see yourself as you really are. Identify the changes you can make in your life, in order to maximize the use of your energy and resources.

The key to being a silent observer lies in being able to observe with no judgement. This means that we do not observe our life and spend the time criticizing ourselves, giving ourself a hard time, or passing remarks about what we are witnessing. We simply observe with no judgement, and with a quiet mind. It is in silent witnessing that we will learn. There is no need to comment at all. Through the simple act of observing, we are learning, interacting and evolving. This is all happening at a deeper level than our logic and rational mind can comprehend.

In order to understand the non-judgemental aspect of this process, it is good to remind ourselves of the intention behind the observation. We may think the intention is to catch ourselves doing it wrong, or getting it wrong, but that is not so. The intention is simply to observe, and at the same time, allow the process of observation to guide us to a deeper level within. This guidance will bring us to a place of experiencing life differently. The healing, learning, and letting go, happens without us even knowing where, when or why. From a true place of silent observation, we begin to bloom at a different pace and at a new level. We will begin to be a different presence in your own world. It is this 'being' that fills us with the resources and the confidence to continue moving through life according to our dreams and visions.

Engaging In 'the process' of moving forward and creating change

1. **Create Your Vision**
   Begin with your dream. When you dream of your future, you are allowing yourself to see what is possible for you. Allow your dream to move from a dream state into a vision for your future. It may seem like semantics or word games, but there is a power in making your dream into your vision. Of course, many often ask how to make a

dream your vision, and the answer is simple, decide that the dream IS your vision.

A dream is something that we often relate to as 'out there'. We often believe that it is unachievable, due to our life conditioning. It is usually connected to being ungrounded, disconnected and removed from this world of practical and measurable realities. A vision, on the other hand, is something that is seen as achievable and definite. It is something that we have our mind set on, our heart connected to, and our confidence weaved throughout. A vision is something that we move towards, and it comes from within us. With that vision foremost in our mind and heart, we know we have the skills, the resources and the capacity to achieve it.

Your vision is the bigger picture of where you are going, and what your life is going to look like once you have set out to make the vision real. In summary, a dream is outside of you and far away, and a vision is something that is within you, a part of you and definitely achievable. Why do you think so many of the world's great thinkers and successful organizations think and act from vision, as opposed to dreams? Visions create movement and happen; dreams create excitement, but generally remain only dreams, stagnant and stuck in the 'out there' realities.

People often make the mistake of trying to make the dream realistic and practical. Dreams are not realistic and they are usually not practical, so dream the dream, but as if you know everything in it can and will be achieved. Don't be realistic or practical. Once the dream is on paper you can go to work to fill in the blanks, add in the details and figure out the challenges. First get the dream on paper, and then begin to reframe it so it becomes your VISION, your plan, your blueprint, and the map of your future. You are not trying to make it happen overnight, nor are you trying to figure out the details. You are painting the bigger picture of your life in the future; a future that starts now and materializes over the coming months and years.

2. *Connect Your Vision and Your Values*

As you set out to create your vision, it is vital that you align it with your values. The vision must be embedded in and with those things that are sacred to you in your life. Are you even aware of what your life values are? Your values are the beliefs you have relative to your life that are non-negotiable. As long as your life is out of sync with your values, you will not find an easy path to creating a life that is peace-filled, achievement-centerd and joyful. The options available to you are peace, achievement and joy, or alternatively, struggle, highs and lows, frustration and disconnectedness. Living according to your deepest values is the only way to settle the ongoing conflict that resides within you. Living according to your values is a choice and in choosing it, you are on the path to self-acceptance. No storm can blow you off that course.

3. *Believe in Your Vision*

Assuming that you have created your vision for your future and that it is aligned with your values (which are clear, prioritized and honest), consider the level of belief that you are living from in relation to the vision. You will only achieve what you believe you can achieve, and those things you do not believe in, will become the breaking points in your plan. They are the holes in the middle of the bridge, the weak links in the chain, and the diversions on the map. They also become your excuse to sabotage yourself and create a drama; this prevents you from moving into a new experience of life.

It is essential that you believe without question that your vision can and *will* be achieved. It is also essential that you learn to catch your negative thought patterns and deal with them. As soon as you begin thinking, 'It can't be done', 'I can't do it', 'This is not realistic' or, 'There is no way to overcome this obstacle', you start to dismantle your vision. You are significantly decreasing your chances of making it across the finish line. In fact, you may accidentally make manifest the negative thought.

What do you think happens to a marathon runner the minute he or she starts to believe she can go no further? The message 'I can't' begins to create a chain reaction throughout that person's world at an emotional, psychological and physical level, and eventually the system weakens to the point that the pain becomes stronger, bigger and more masterful, than the belief in being able to finish. The mind can trap you in thought patterns, and when you most need to escape from them, you find that you are simply too far into the negativity to find the strength to get out. At that moment, you convince yourself that the only way to get out is to stop and quit.

When you believe you can, you will find a way to support that belief and make it work, but you need to 'believe'. Keep on believing, and then believe some more, until one day you wake up with a confidence so strong that nothing will cause you to question yourself ever again, the path you're on, or the destination you are moving towards.

Belief is the fire cracker that gets you moving, and once you are moving, you simply need to reinforce the belief to gather the momentum you need to break through every barrier that stands in your way. There is nothing as great as a moment of breakthrough. It is that moment that shows you, teaches you and empowers you to know that you can achieve whatever vision you pursue.

4. *Create Leverage*
In order to remain focused and in a state of belief, it is important that you have what is referred to as leverage. Leverage could be described as influence, power, force, control, pull and weight. You are using leverage to manipulate (in the positive sense) your mindset, in order to remain in the psychological state necessary to achieve

your end goal. In the bigger picture, this end goal is your vision, but in the shorter term, leverage is used to keep you focused on all of the smaller goals that you are moving towards. You must be able to achieve all of the smaller goals in order to realize the bigger picture. You can create leverage by focusing on the positive and negative outcomes in relation to your goal(s). The following are powerful questions to ask yourself, and when answered with emotion, passion and color (detail), give you plenty of reasons to remain focused and in a state of belief.

Using the positive to create leverage:

1. What will my day be like if I remain steadfast in my goal?
2. What will my life be like when I achieve my objectives?
3. Who will I become in remaining strong and focused on the path to my dreams?
4. What will I be teaching my children and those I love, by sticking it out and creating the success I dream of?
5. What is the sense of self that I will have by allowing my dreams and vision to be realized?

Using the negative to create leverage:

1. What will my day be like if I do NOT remain steadfast in my goals?
2. What will my life be like if I do NOT allow myself to achieve my dreams and realize my vision?

3. Who will I become if I GIVE UP on myself?
4. What will I be teaching my children and those I love, if I do NOT stick with my dreams, goals and vision?
5. What is the sense of self that I will have by NOT allowing my dreams and visions to be realized?

By answering these questions in full and having real emotion, passion and detail in your answer, you are giving yourself:

>   --The influence needed to convince you to keep going.
>   --A reminder of the power of the vision and the 'why' behind your actions.
>   --The force you need to move you through the moments of doubt and questioning.
>   --The sense of control you need to remember that you are 'the boss' of your life and the creator of your future.
>   --The pull you need to get through a tough day when you feel you do not have the strength to do it on your own.
>   --The weight needed to reinforce your belief that the goals you have set out to achieve are realistic and possible.

Remember, creating leverage is not something you do just once. You must revisit your focus often, every day if necessary, until it becomes automatic or until you have achieved your outcome. The playing field of life can be an amusing, difficult and a challenging place to be. Every day you may be subject to people, situations, circumstances and events that will try to pull you off course, and suck you into the game of life that keeps people disempowered, upset, downbeat and submissive. There may be days when you feel like it is just you against the world, and that there is no one and nothing there to support you, encourage you or motivate you. It is sad to say that when these days come, they are powerful influencers, because often the world will not want to see you succeed. There are a few points to highlight in relation to this:

--**Expectations**: If you have high expectations of the world around you helping you to achieve your goals, you are at risk of being deeply disappointed. Believe in yourself, ask for help, but do not be disheartened if it is not forthcoming. Also, do not put all of your trust in anything or anyone but yourself.

--**The 'Norm'**: Setting out to achieve your own success by yourself and for yourself is not the norm for many people. Therefore, they may not understand, and have an adverse reaction to your new way of being. Make your new way your norm and allow everybody else to have theirs; but don't play on their playing field or you risk getting caught up in their negativity.

--**The Tribe**: It is not unusual for the actions of an independent thinker to challenge others in the tribe (family and friends) to do the same for themselves. However, if they are afraid of failure or stuck in negativity, they may consciously or unconsciously, try to sabotage you and your vision. This is usually in an attempt to remove the pressure they feel from your empowerment.

--**Culture**: If you come from a culture that is not primarily one of motivation, independence, and positivity about success, there is a risk that the cultural norm will try to dismantle you and your vision. You need to remain strong and focused.

--**Fear**: Many people are afraid 'for you', so out of 'love' (or what they think is love), they may tell you everything that can and will go wrong. Develop the art of selective listening.

--**Ignorance**: Many people live in a state of ignorance and under the influence of emotional, psychological and spiritual anaesthesia. From this place of not knowing, people often try to convince others that they are stupid to try to succeed where many have failed.

--**Jealousy**: Sadly, there are people in the world who would rather see you fail, especially if they feel their own life is not the success they had desired. These people are neither friend nor enemy. They are simply lost, disappointed and angry with life. They don't want to see anyone succeed, unless they too, are succeeding and they rarely are.

--**Aggression**: Many people who have been hurt in life hold a lot of aggression within them. Aggression is a powerful energy force and, if directed at you, can do serious damage to morale and energy levels. Learn to be like the Samurai warrior and stay calm, centerd and in control of your own thoughts and actions at all times.

--**Control**: People often feel the need to be in control of something. If they are not feeling that they are in control of their life, they may try to take control of your life, your vision and your plans. Stay strong in who you are, what you are doing, why you are doing it, and keep reminding yourself of these things.

There are ways to deal with these threats to your vision, and I offer the following suggestions for you to practice:

--Spend your time with people who support, encourage and help you.
--Keep your ideas and your plans secret until they and you are strong enough to stand up to criticism.
--Keep reminding yourself of the answers to the 'leverage questions' that were just mentioned and take nothing personally.
--In the words of my wise and wonderful father, 'Keep your head down, ass up, and plough on!'

Contradiction # 4

Letting Go Means Holding On

How many times in your life have you heard someone telling you to 'let go'? It seems to be one of those popular sayings that everyone loves to use. However, while letting go can be a powerful experience, it is important to know:

1. In order to let go you must hold on.
2. It is good to know what to hold on to, in order to know what to let go of, and of course, survive the letting go.

Even the man who chooses to live as a hermit (and in doing so appears to let go of everything) holds onto a number of things. He holds onto the understanding that it is best for him to be alone at that stage in his life. It is his belief that solitude allows him to access a certain level of being, and that he may not achieve it with other people around. He holds onto his map of the world and chooses to see it as a better way of life, at least for now. His letting go is only possible by his holding on. Letting go and holding on are two sides of the same coin. It is having an understanding of who you are, what you want, and what your life is really about, that makes things easier and possible. Do you know the answer to the question of who you are? If not, don't panic or worry, the beauty of life is that you can be whoever you need to be. In other words, you choose who you are and you decide what your purpose is.

You must balance the concept of letting go, with knowing that you will always be holding on to something that allows you to experience what 'letting go' is really about. A person who simply lets go with no awareness, is going to find themselves trying to navigate through the world without direction, without meaning, understanding, or a sense of purpose.

Walking Away vs. Letting Go

It is important to know the difference between walking away and letting go. In most cases, what we really need to let go of is a 'frame of mind', a 'way of thinking', a 'perception' or a 'certain map of the world'. Sometimes moving on in life may mean enormous changes in terms of relationships, jobs, or place of residence. Furthermore, it can be healthy to let go of our old ways of *thinking,* before dropping other elements of our life.

Even if we do change major aspects of our life, but don't change our thinking, the likelihood is that in the new relationship, new job, or new home, we will once again recreate old patterns, old behaviors, and old perceptions. On the other hand, you may be amazed at what happens in the world around you when the world *within* you has changed.

Once we have transformed our way of thinking, we may discover that there are changes required in more of the practical elements of life. With a new way of thinking, we can see the changes needed from a new place and with a new understanding. Only then will we have the resources needed to improve our life and reduce, if not eliminate, negative fallout and potentially destructive results.

Remember, the way we think today is a result of how we have experienced life up until now, and also what we believe to be true or false, right or wrong. Change these beliefs and everything changes.

Being True to Yourself
You are the only person you need to be true to as you move through life. The more truth there is within you and in the world around you, the more likely it is that you will find new levels of peace and comfort. Being true to yourself is not limited to your inner dialogue and beliefs. It involves action; it involves how you dream and what you dream; and it involves how you interact with the world.

In addition, if you are being true to yourself, then there is a part of you, a silent observer, who is ever vigilant and conscious of the implications of your intentions and your actions.

The journey of being true to yourself requires a continual assessment of your life. You do not simply 'check in' with yourself once every so often – you 'check in' all the time. Considering that life is constantly changing, moving and evolving, it is fair to say that you too, are constantly changing, moving and evolving. You are not the same person today that you were six months ago or five years ago, and you will not be the same person tomorrow that you are today. Being true to yourself is *a way of life* that requires regular 'checking in'.

There is a 'you' in the word 'yourself'. You will find it difficult to be true to yourself unless you know who *you* are. Do you know who you are? Where you came from? What is the purpose of this life you have? What is the meaning of being here? Why are things the way they are for *you*?

Assuming you do want to be true to yourself, what is the context in which you want to know this truth? Do you want to be true to:

1. An image you have of the person you should be in terms of work, having a family, saving for a rainy day, building a big pension?
2. Do you want to be true to something deeper, more meaningful; perhaps more mystical and mysterious; something that connects you to parts of our world that exist, but cannot be seen; parts that are there to be experienced as much as the everyday life we know?

When you go on a journey to find your truth, there is nowhere to hide. All hidden aspects of you need to be considered, exposed, challenged and met face-to-face. Being true to yourself means tapping into what makes you great, but it also means tapping into the pain, the wounds, the fear, the hurt and the sadness. It is a beautiful journey and one that is filled with many moments of healing and connection that are powerful beyond description.

Releasing the Emotion

Emotions are very powerful. Facing the emotions that we have been keeping at bay for a long time, can be one of the most difficult things we ever have to do. There seems to be something within that quietly chatters at us and warns us of the bad things that 'might' happen if we release our true and honest feelings.

This inner chatter draws from the many moments of fear and the experiences you have had in the past. It may be the voice of society saying, 'Be careful'; the voice of a parent saying, 'just get up and get on with it'; or the voice of an old teacher telling you not to speak until you are spoken to. It may be a memory of being laughed at or humiliated the last time you tried to speak of your feelings. Perhaps the voice is one of fear because you simply don't believe you can explain the truth of what is going on within you. It may be that part of you is afraid to let go of your hurt and painful emotions. After all, who would you be without your pain, without your hurt, without your drama? Who would you be without your 'story'?

It is vital that you release the blocked emotions that are within you. If you don't, these blocks will simply cause the pain to grow. They will fester, grow, mutate and, as time goes by, they can become totally debilitating. There is only one person who can face, challenge and heal these emotions, and that is you. There is no coach, healer or master that can do it for you. They may offer support and assistance, but only you can heal your wounds. You choose to hurt and you also are the one that chooses to heal.

Let's not assume that it's a negative or bad thing to have emotions that require healing. If you're hurt, wounded or in a negative place emotionally, you are not flawed, broken or 'less than' what you could be, you are simply alive. There is no perfect state, so there is no need to look for it. There is only this moment, and this moment is neither good nor bad; it simply is.

Releasing an emotion doesn't mean getting rid of it; it simply means learning about it, and discovering aspects of it, of which you were not aware. You will learn to navigate life in such a way that you are the master of the emotion, and the emotion does not become your master. The idea of releasing emotions is one of learning to allow flow in your life. When you allow the emotions to flow, you are allowing yourself to experience life with less work, effort and without the exhaustion. Learn to value all emotions. They are teachers; become your own student.

The Boomerang Effect
Whatever you send out to the world will come back to you. Even though you bury certain emotions, eventually you will have to face and deal with them. You cannot avoid dealing with them, but you *can* decide how to experience or process these emotions.

A person who has a lot of anger within them will most likely spend their life dealing with a world that is angry. They will

74

experience people that are angry, traffic that is aggressive, relationships that are hostile, and money challenges that create anger. What is within you is all you will see most of the time, in the world around you. A person that is filled with the emotion of loneliness will most likely spend a lot of their life dealing with loneliness in the world around them. Everywhere they look they will see realities that echo what is going on within them. A person who is filled with fear will see only things in the world that will create more fear. They will experience fear to the point of being unable to move forward or unable to overcome life's challenges.

The world around you is mostly an illusion and the illusion is created and reinforced by your projections. It doesn't matter whether you believe that or not. There are universal laws at play and they do their thing, regardless of whether or not you believe in them. However, making the choice to believe in certain universal realities will offer you opportunities and possibilities that you couldn't have had by remaining ignorant of these truths.

What signals are you sending out to the world? Consider how the world interacts with you. What challenges do you seem to be faced with most of the time? Be honest with how you see life and the world around you. Whatever it is that you see is most likely the same thing that you are putting out there. This can be a hard thing to accept. Notice how you are feeling when you think about this. If this law is true, then are you sending out what you want to get back?

A Shock to the System

Healing time and attention to pain are an essential part of achieving a true level of inner peace, and this can be a shock to the system. It is about knowing life at the most fundamental level. If the healing process is not challenging you and creating a whole new perspective on life, it is most likely not a real healing. There are a number of aspects or phases of healing that you will go through as you create a new life experience:

--Compassionate healing on an emotional level
--Challenging healing on an intellectual level
--Spiritual healing on a soul/spirit level
--The healing of the body on a physical level

There is much more to you than the way you think and how you feel. You experience life through many different 'bodies'; all of these bodies interact with each other; and each of these interactions make up an aspect or element of the complete program that you are both uploading and downloading. It is this process that contributes to how you choose to perceive life and, in turn, this perception creates the experience you have, as well as the reality you live in.

Let's say for now, that life is not what you think, and you are not what you think. What you think is most likely connected to your subjective understanding of what reality is, which isn't necessarily correct. It is simply an element or an aspect of reality. You could argue that it is reality, but it is not all that life has to offer.

'Authentic' healing, manifestation, and self-awareness, require you to go on an authentic journey to the inner realms of self. I call this 'The Journey Home'. On this journey, you are stripped of everything that you once believed you were and you experience that which you are. It can be a frightening journey but, once traveled, you will know your heart and your place in this world, in a way you have never known. You will know peace and you will become peace.

Can you do this part-time?

'No, you cannot do this part-time.' In order to create, you must become the creator, and that is a full-time commitment, a full-time job and a full-time process. It is *a way of life,* and nothing less.

If letting go means holding on, what do we hold on to?

This is a great question to ask yourself in life. What do I hold on to? It seems that, as we move through the years, many of us ask this question simply because we begin to experience the impermanence of most things, and some people have even ventured out far enough to realize that everything is impermanent. There is only one thing you need to hold onto, and in holding on to this one thing, you will eliminate the need to get caught up, bogged down, frustrated, stressed, worried or anxious about anything. Take a moment to ask yourself what worries you most in life and make a list. If you are like most of the population on this planet, you will see that most of the worries on your list center around things you can do nothing about, and/or have no control over. The answer is, hold on to *nothing.*

One of the most empowering decisions in life is to let go of all the things in ourselves (and around us) that no longer serve us. In doing so, we give ourselves the gift of space, time, peace, opportunity, freedom, self-worth and confidence needed to fully experience life.

This is not to say that you walk away from your life, leave your spouse, shut up the house, axe the job, and head for the hills. However, it does demand that you relinquish all *attachment* to them, and you see them as only aspects of life, not anything that defines life or who you are. By holding onto nothing, you are living from a consciousness of the present moment. You are valuing only what is within you, knowing that the drama and madness of the world is an illusion. It is only then that you are living from a consciousness of confidence. This kind of confidence continually informs you that everything is exactly as it is meant to be. From this awareness you remain focused on the present moment, and you do not get caught up in the fear of the future, the shame of the past, or the anxiety of thinking you are not enough.

Nothing is something.
By holding onto nothing, which is the ultimate letting go, you are holding onto everything that matters most. From nothing comes everything. By realizing this, and jumping into the void that we call nothing, you are in fact allowing the true nature of life itself, to provide for you with a limitless abundance. In letting go, you can be confident in knowing that everything you need will come to you. It doesn't matter whether it is money, relationships, time

off, a home, food, or friends. All these things are yours, and all you need to do is claim them by living from the confidence that assures you of that. Of course, by holding onto nothing, you are bringing these things into your life. They are only for the purpose of experiencing them, therefore, they do not give you your identity. From that consciousness, you are free to enjoy them without the fear of losing them.

Engaging in 'the process' of moving forward and holding on to let go

1. Write out in a clear and positive context the change that you want to see happening in your life.
2. List the things, people and circumstances that will support you as you let go.
3. List the things, people and circumstances that will stand against you and/or limit you as you let go.
4. Identify what needs to happen to overcome the limiting factors as they arise. This may include people who can help you through any resistance you meet.
5. Identify all fears coming from your life experience that will prevent you from letting go and taking the risk needed to create the life you want.
6. Identify what you need to do to overcome these fears before they arise.
7. Identify the biggest step you are required to take to ensure that the process of change has begun, and to know that there is no turning back.

8. Take that step as soon as possible. Identify the date and time that you will do it. Do not make it a date and time too far into the future or it will never happen.

9. Let go of everything that brings to mind an insecurity or a fear, and hold on to only that which encourages and motivates you to continue on your new path. Keep going no matter what happens.

Contradiction # 5

Slow Down To Go Faster

We all get busy in life, move fast, take on many challenges and keep moving in what we believe to be the right direction. We are all looking for peace, less work, more time for ourselves and a little slice of happiness, only to wake up every morning in the same life we had the day before.

The very nature of moving at a fast pace and doing a lot, keeps us from slowing down and having peace. By moving fast we are bypassing the option for an easy life, one that offers less work and more time. How can we expect to have time off if our focus is on getting so much done? How can we expect to find peace if our world is filled with chaos and deadlines? How can we ever sit still, if the life we've created is demanding that we are always on the go?

It isn't a matter of restructuring and behaving differently, although these activities do enter the equation. It is more a matter of deconstructing and rebuilding life with a new focus, and from a new belief system. The only way to find peace is to move away from all that causes disruption. Then allow time for all that creates the very peace you seek.

Peace is felt as a result of what we do. What we do is built from what we believe and where we 'place our hat' in life. If the priority is to get rich and have a masterful life of luxury, then it is likely, in most cases, that you will be busy until you die, never having a substantial amount of time to actually enjoy what you have created. If, however, you have a desire to create a life experience that allows you the time to stop and smell the roses, you will be called to live in a very different way.

Slowing Down

Most of the time, people are busy with things that are unnecessary. Slowing down in life means allowing yourself to be honest enough to see what is not necessary, and then begin to live with your attention firmly on the things that matter and nothing more. It is the most wonderful and exciting thing you can do for yourself. Examine what in your life is burning up your energy, your vision, and getting in your way. Then force yourself to stop. If you do not take the necessary steps to change your life, you will die in the same pattern that you are living today. You will see things tomorrow the same as you saw them yesterday. No one can do it for you.

To slow down in some cases, means to stop. Learn to say no, learn to walk away, learn how to disengage, learn to keep what matters most firmly in sight. Do what manifests your life purpose according to your own judgement and measurement.

Going Faster

Once we have learned to slow down in life, we will get where we want to go a lot easier and a lot faster. Slowing down removes all the obstacles that prevent us from reaching our destination! Slowing down allows us to cruise through our day while the people around us remain caught up in their entanglements. This is because they are moving through their day according to someone else's idea of what is right and wrong for them.

By slowing down and not allowing oursleves to become tied up in the dramas of life, we create the space, the time, the clarity and the capacity to see a lot more. Once we see where we are going, there is a much better chance of actually getting there.

Think of the sixty-two year old woman who dreams of opening a healing center. She is broke and spending the little money she has traveling around in the hope of meeting the people that she thinks will fund her project. What happened, that at sixty-two she is still trying to achieve something that began as a dream over twenty years ago? She was too busy with all of life's other stuff, and got caught up in playing the game and obeying the rules. Erroneously, she was stuck in the belief that she had to do a number of things before she would be able to move on to her dream. Twenty years later, the other stuff is still not done, and she is still hoping for something that is not likely to happen unless something changes. Otherwise, the odds are stacked against her to the point that, even if she were to manage to make her dream come true, it might be short lived. You simply cannot sit and bask in the sun when you are busy digging trenches in the rain.

Stop doing what is not creating your dream, and you will significantly increase the chances of actualizing the dream. Slow down to move faster, or else the alternative is to keep going as you are. Which do you think is most likely to help you get where you really want to go?

The Challenge in Slowing Down
Take time to go within and examine yourself for any of this negative self-talk:

Fear of getting it wrong
I will look bad, others will judge me. I'm different, therefore I will not be good enough. Life is about getting it right; no one likes people who get it wrong....

Fear of upsetting someone
I will be judged, they will be upset with me. I will get in trouble and they will not like me. I will not be good enough for them to like me....

Fear of letting others down
They will not be able to trust me, therefore I will not be trusted. I do not measure up, therefore, I will not be given another chance; they will see me as not being capable. I will be the reason they feel bad, they will not like me for this.....

Fear of not having enough
I am not like others who have these things, so I will not belong. I will not be welcome, I will not be enough or have enough to be recognized as one of them....

Fear of being alone

Being alone means I got it wrong. I am alone because I have made mistakes and was not able to get things right. I am not good enough to have others in my life, no one likes me....

Fear of experiencing pain

Pain only happens when something has gone wrong. Pain makes me feel like I have no strength. Pain is what happens to bad people. I am not able to manage pain, I cannot cope with pain. Pain might kill me and my life will end in misery....

Fear of losing what you have

If I lose what I have, I have failed. Successful people have plenty; if I have little I am not successful. Losing what I have will upset me, and then no one will want to be around me. Losing what I have is a sign that I am not able, capable and good enough to have what others can have and keep....

Fear of getting lost

Having no direction is a sign that I am a failure. Being lost happens to people who have nothing to offer. Lost is a sign of weakness; if I get lost, I am different from all those who are not lost. How come everyone else seems to know where they are going, what they want, and are getting it? What is wrong with me?....

Fear of not being loved

I cannot be loved because I know I am not good enough. Being loved will cause me to live a lie, because I am not able to give back all that love. I cannot love very well and I don't love myself very much; I am flawed and not perfect. Love only happens to people who deserve it, and I do not deserve it. I am not good enough for love....

Fear of not belonging
I am different; I am not like everyone else. Knowing that I do not belong just tells me that I am lost and without direction. I have little to offer to anyone anyway. If I were better than I am at my job or my relationship I would belong here, but because I am not like others, I don't really belong here. I can't do it; I'm not good enough.... I don't deserve to belong....

Fear of not knowing what you should know
Everybody else seems to know these things, what is wrong with me? Why am I so naïve? I am not as smart as they are. I can't do it as well as they can. What if I get it wrong? I should know this; they will think I am stupid....

Fear of misleading others
What if I am wrong and I mislead them? They will be angry with me. I will be responsible; I will get in trouble; they will not like me; they might even laugh at me; they won't believe me anymore; no one will trust me because I can't get it right most of the time....

Fear of responsibility
I am responsible for them and their happiness. What if I get it wrong and cause them to be unhappy, mad, disappointed, upset

or angry? They will be angry with me; I am not enough and do not know enough to be confident that I can do this....

Fear of being unattractive

If I am not attractive they will not want me around; if I do not look the part I will not fit in; people make judgments about looks and I am not as attractive as they are. If I don't look good they will not take me seriously. I will not get the part; do I look stupid, fat, ugly, sad, lost?....

Fear of letting go

If I let this go what will I have? Without this I will feel like I don't have anything; this is too important to me; I am not good enough to get this back; having to let go will tell me that I got it wrong in the first place; why do I keep getting it wrong? What is wrong with me?....

Fear of holding on

If I hold on to this I will have to accept that wanting to let go was me giving up; holding on means commitment and I am not ready for commitment; I always get it wrong; best to just let it go and start again; holding on will make me face up to what is upsetting me; I can't solve this....

Fear of the unknown

What if something goes wrong? I want a sure thing. What if I can't handle it? Maybe I won't be able to cope; I have got things wrong so much in the past and it will happen again; I'm scared and unsure of myself; I don't have the confidence to do it or to go there....

Fear of failure

If I get it wrong people won't like me; it will cause problems for others; I will only make a bad situation worse; it is better to do nothing than get it wrong; I don't have what it takes to make it work; what happens if something I cannot deal with comes along and makes a mess of everything?....

Fear of success

People will look to me for answers; what if I don't have them? What will I get myself into by taking on more than I can handle? I will be discovered as a fraud; it won't last and I will look like a fool; I am not good enough to have this success, or for it to be real; something will go wrong and I will end up worse off than I am now....

Fear of not being noticed

No one listens to me; what I have to say is unimportant. If they don't recognize me, I will have little meaning; people who are noticed are the people who get the chances and make the difference; there are so many other people wanting this so I need to be unique and visible; I will be left on my own with nothing if they do not recognize me and if I don't get the opportunity....

Fear of God

I will be in trouble if I even think that thought; I am letting God down, He who loves me; I am running the risk of being sent to hell, if I do not get it right; God is watching me and sees when I screw up; he will judge me. God will not let me have that in my life because of how selfish I have been. I need to put others before myself; I need to stop wanting so much for me....

Fear of regret

What if I wake up one day wondering and regretting? If I don't do this I will be sorry; I don't want to have to deal with knowing that I got it wrong; doing this (or not doing this) will make me feel beaten and wrong; I can't afford to let my guard down; what will others think?....

Fear of saying no

They will not like me; I don't want to upset them; I will feel like I am being selfish and non-supportive if I refuse; what if saying no makes them angry and they do not want to be around me anymore? What if I say no and I regret it in the future?...I will feel guilty for letting them down.

Fear of love

Who would I be without my drama? Being loved and allowing the love would tell me that I have been hard on myself and wrong in the past; loving myself means being okay with everything as it is, but that's not possible because there is so much that needs improving and changing; it's not that easy....

Fear of receiving

If I take this, they will think I am a 'sponger'; I am not good enough to take this; I do not deserve this; others need this more than I do; I am not the right person for that; it makes me uncomfortable to accept and receive gifts...

Fear of giving

If I give I will be left with nothing; giving is not something I can do easily; they/the world owes me something; I am keeping what I have or I will be left with nothing; I have given in the past and gotten nothing back, so I'm not taking any chances or making that mistake again; I don't have any extra or enough to give....

Fear of believing in self

It cannot all be up to me; there must be something else that makes this possible; I do not have total power or control over my life; how could that be? Who will I blame if it all goes wrong? This would mean that I am totally responsible for my life; I couldn't be, because there are so many others in my life that affect my choices. I am not all that strong and powerful; there has to be a catch, it is not that easy....

Fear of truth

I would rather stay in the illusion a little longer; the truth might be good, but it will bring with it a demand for change; if I allow the things that I am not ready to accept, I might not be able to handle it. Knowing the truth will make it difficult; once I know the truth, there is no 'not knowing it', and I can't go back. What if it changes my mind or causes me to see things and people differently?....

Fear of change

Things may not be perfect, but at least I am familiar with life as it is; I know how to handle life in its current form; what if the change brings situations and circumstances that are beyond my control? I don't want to go through more change; I have had enough change to last a lifetime; I just want to have some certainty for a while....

Fear of confrontation

I don't want to feel responsible and deal with this thing; I am scared of what this means; I don't know if I understand the truth of this and how to deal with it; confrontation means that I am being challenged; what if I am not up to the challenge and am unable to defend my perspective of the situation? What if I am discovered as being wrong?....

Fear of acceptance

I don't know what this really means, accept what? To accept means that I have given up my view on situations; does this mean that I was wrong? What might people think of me if they discover that I was wrong? Why can't others accept what I have to say and let go of their beliefs instead?....

Fear of allowing

If I allow things to be this way I will have no power; what if I get it wrong and allowing this causes me more discomfort? If I just allow this to be, who is in control, if it isn't me? What happens next? Does what I have to say have any significance?....

Fear of ill health

What if I get sick, lose my health, or get injured? Bad health means that I am finished and my destiny is in the hands of the gods; being ill is a sign of weakness and being beaten; being sick means that I cannot achieve what I want in my life, I would probably die and it would be over….

Fear of risk

If I take this risk and it doesn't work, I will end up worse off than I am now; it is better not to take risks because I might look like a fool if it doesn't work out; it is better to be safe than sorry; taking risks only leads to disappointment; risks are foolish and only create bigger problems; I have responsibilities and I cannot take this risk….

Fear of not being a victim

If I stop blaming other people and situations for my circumstances, that means that this is all my fault and I am to blame; but I didn't do this, it is not my fault, I have been unlucky; I just keep making the wrong decisions; too many people have influenced me to the point that I can't seem to get it right; I am not good enough to be happy and worry free….

Fear of dying

Where will I go? What has this all been about? I am so disappointed; did my life really mean anything? What about the people I leave behind? I don't want them to be upset with me, and I can't bear the thought of them being unhappy if I leave this earth. Will everyone forget about me?....

Of course, by now you realize that all of the challenges of letting go, slowing down, and changing the way we live are linked to a 'FEAR'. There is little else except for your own fear, that can get in your way. Those who are afraid don't and those that are not afraid do. You are either doing it or you are not, there is no in between, no matter what anybody tells you.

Which of these fears apply to you, or do they all to one extent or another? What needs to happen for you to overcome that fear? When are you going to allow yourself to do it? And if not now, when? If not you, who? What excuse are you holding onto? What is the pain you are avoiding going through? For what reason do you prefer to remain in the pain?

What do you need? This question can be a real trap for some people. It is not unusual for them to answer with a wish list of things they 'know' are needed, in order to get where they want to go. However, if the list you write has anything in it that is of a material reality, you are most likely missing the entire point. The 'what I need' list that holds the most punch, power and possibility is a list of the things you need from within yourself. They can be given to you only by you. What might some of these things be? If you do find that there are material things on your list simply go through the list one at a time and ask, 'How can I give this to myself?'

The game of life is a beautiful dance of movements that will bring you to the realization that you are on your own; it is up to you, you don't need anyone else, and you are the one. Of course this is true unless, it is not.

Be Where You Are

Be here now, there is nowhere else to be. If you are not here, where are you? Every day will bring you an invitation to be fully

93

present in that day. This is an invitation not to drift off into the things of the past, nor to get lost in the hopes of the future. As long as you believe that the past, the future, or any other place you can create in your imagination, is more important than the here and now, it is likely that you will continue to go there. That is fine, unless it is not. You need to ask 'where do I need to be in order to experience life?' The answer is simple; you need to be where you are. There is little point in being where you are not, if what you need is where you are.

Trying to get anywhere without being in the present is futile and on all occasions, ends in sadness, frustration, upset and a deep dive into the spiral of distance from the self. Everything is here, that is the nature of life. Everything is in the now, that is the nature of being; everything is as it is, that is the nature of everything. Fighting nature is not a good thing. It is better to spend your time understanding this than trying to create that which cannot be, unless of course, it is not. Everything is what it is, and nothing is what it seems.

Engaging In 'the process' of slowing down to go faster

1. Write down on a sheet of paper in no more than one hundred words, a description of the life you are currently living. Be honest, authentic and heartfelt.
2. Write under that, a description of the life you want to experience.
3. Write a list, as long as is needed, that highlights all the differences in both descriptions.

4. On a clean sheet of paper, write out each answer from number three again, one at a time, and as you go through them write after the answer, what is needed emotionally, psychologically, spiritually, and physically, for you to achieve a change towards the positive in relation to that item.

5. After each answer to number four list the people you know that can offer you the support you need to make that happen.

6. After each answer to number five identify what might possibly happen, that will get in the way of the change you desire to take place.

7. After each answer to number six, identify what is needed to overcome the possible barrier, resistance or challenge that you are preparing for.

8. After each answer to number seven, identify one action you can take within the next 24 hours that will get you started on the journey of creating the change needed.

9. Take the action.

10. Stop doing everything else.

Contradiction # 6

Failure is Success

Failure means we have failed, unless it doesn't. Along the way, 'mistakes' are made, some things don't work out, significant failures happen, and there are moments when everything gets lost. It may seem that we have taken one step forward and two steps back. These things don't happen because we have done wrong, because we are stupid, or because we don't deserve for things to work out. They happen as a direct result of the choices we make. That is life, and that is the way it is supposed to play out. All that happens is a result of our own creation, so there must be something in the 'setbacks' that we knew we needed. Why else would we create them?

The Madness of Needing Failure
There is nothing mad about creating a life situation that hasn't worked out. In fact, it is these moments that can become our most precious gems. Life is a process of learning, a process of remembering, and a process of realization. How can you even begin to think that something can happen without a deep and meaningful reality behind it?

Imagine that there are two parts to you; one part knows everything, it knows who you are, where you are from, what your purpose is, why you are here, and what is needed in order for you to find your way home. This part of you knows the journey you are on, and it knows the correct steps you need to take in order for it all to make sense. This is what will give peace its rightful place as master of your life.

The other part of you is the part that lives in this world, doing the things that this world says you must do, and demanding certain actions from you, in order for you to fit into societies 'righteousness'.

Imagine that you are living with two guides, two powerful forces that want you to live according to their understanding of what you need. Let's call them 'The Heart Self' and 'The Head Self'. The heart-self knows all there is to know and by virtue of that fact, it can find a way through every life situation that you create. The head-self knows only what it has learned and therefore, it often finds itself stuck in a cul-de-sac, with nowhere to go. How can it know what it does not yet know?

The heart-self knows how you learn, what your process is, and the patterns you live by. It has only one agenda, and that is to help you to remember who you are, to guide you home, and to show you that everything is perfect just the way it is. This perfection exists now, there is nowhere else. You're all-knowing self will take you where you need to be in order to remember. Most of the time this remembering will happen as a result of explicit moments we experience in this thing called life. This all-knowing self, the 'heart' self, also trusts you without question. It knows that you will go where you need to go, and remember in order to learn and grow.

Your mind also knows what you need but it does not necessarily know that it knows it. This part of you lives with doubt, and that doubt has been learned, reinforced, and encouraged in many ways throughout life. The doubt often shows up in trust issues, confidence issues, and a sense of not being enough. These feelings often trick us into thinking that we are not yet complete. We feel we are inadequate and struggle for peace and confidence. However, the heart-self knows that you are fully capable and it guides you, as you explore your own negative feelings. This allows you to have the necessary experiences that show you that you are there already.

We spend all of our time alternating between these two selves without realizing it. We don't allow ourselves to grasp the fact that these two parts of the self have their own way of doing things. When we accept this as fact and just 'allow' it, both parts can be great teachers, great givers of wisdom, and great guides. Instead we simply think that everything is part of the one. Although everything is one, you cannot exclude the essential part of oneness, known to us as 'duality'. Nor can you exclude the important aspect of duality, which is oneness. Both exist as one and separate.

The challenge we are faced with is the challenge of ignorance. We often do not stop long enough in life to search for an understanding of the fundamentals, an experience, or even an indication of our true nature. It is the part that is unaware, that allows us to be who we are, go where we feel we need to go, and do what we think we need to do, even if that means disaster. Why? Because this is who we are, how we learn, and it is simply the way we do things. We will continue to do things this way until the time comes that we don't.

How does all this fit into the discussion about failure? This tells us that there is no failure; there is only the road we take in order to learn what we need to learn. In this way, we have a choice in choosing not just an easier road, but a different road the next time. This is because you will have learned the lessons this time, unless you haven't. Even if you choose not to learn them, there is no need for concern, as you are starting to realize that everything is exactly as it should be. Remember, what you call mistakes in this journey of life are not really mistakes at all, they are just moments on the road of learning, remembering and realizing. It is not mad to need failure, it is mad to think you don't need it.

In order to succeed,
you will fail many times.

In order to fail many times,
you will need to remain focused on your success.

In order to remain focused on your success,
you will need to allow the failure to happen
without resistance.

In order to allow failure to happen,
you will need to make it an important part
of your success plan.

In order to include failure in your success plan,
you will need to strive from your heart, not your
head.

In order to strive from your heart,
you will need to love your vision.

In order to love your vision,
you will need to accept the fact
that all visions are filled with flaws.

In order to accept the flaws,
you will need to be detached from how
things ought to be.

In order to be detached,
you will need to know that all is
as it is meant to be.

In order to know that all is as it is meant to be,
you will need to know that you are
just as you are meant to be.

In order to know that you are
just as you are meant to be,

you will need to accept that
you are perfect right now.

In order to know that you are perfect,
you will need to see that failure
is also a part of perfection.

When you know that failure
is a part of your perfection,
you will welcome it.

When you welcome failure,
you will learn to love the journey
and success will no longer matter.

When you have achieved this,
you have attained the ultimate success.

The Fear of Success

For most of us, the fear of success has a bigger impact on life than the fear of failure. The fear of success is not necessarily a fear of achieving your dream, nor do I believe that it is a fear of creating the change that is required. The fear of success has more to do with the fear of who you will be once you have reached your goal. Most of this happens at a deep subconscious level, but none the less, it happens, and the results can be powerful; so powerful that they can cause people to remain in their slumber and give up on their dreams.

Successful people (by successful, I am referring to authentic success and not success measured by money or possessions alone) are people who are happy within themselves. They live in peace and they spend their lives allowing life to have its say and make its contribution. They don't blame, judge, point the finger, resort to defense mechanisms, live from anger, project, transfer, or use people or things as the reason for the circumstances in their lives.

To be living from success means living from a new consciousness and a new understanding of who you are. The old mindset cannot understand how 'you' can be without your burdens, your pains, your sabotage and your defenses. Therefore, it continually brings up cautions and alarm bells advising you to be careful. It simply cannot compute the two worlds and how they can live in harmony. That is because they cannot live in harmony. Only one can exist in your life at any one time; so you are either living from and in your failure (a sense of 'not enough') or from and in your success (a sense that everything is perfect as it is). Remember that the courage to be successful comes from achieving the success, not before it. The only thing you need to do is to progress through the resistance. Find the feeling and follow it, for it will take you to where you need to go.

Being Hard on Yourself

There is a big difference in being hard on yourself and refusing to allow yourself to stray from your life's path. What separates them is intention.

You are being hard on yourself if the intention behind it is any of the following:
--an intolerance of any mistakes
--to be forceful in order to keep yourself present
--you are living from a consciousness of little, if any, leniency
--you are not living in the present moment, or enjoying the learning process.
--your eyes are always looking to the future, firmly set on the destination. This is exhausting to say the least.

The main motivation for movement comes from our inner critic. The memories of life from our data bank have taught us about punishment and the price that would be paid for getting things wrong, for not completing something, and for being indifferent to those around us.

On the other hand, not allowing yourself to stray from your chosen path is a decision that comes from a place of love, compassion, respect, deserving, growth and peace. With the mindset that you will not allow yourself to drift, you are staying focused on loving yourself. This means loving yourself enough to finally achieve the peace that you have searched so hard to find. The language used from the inner voice is gentle, compassionate, and focused on progress for the purpose of peace and empowerment, in terms of learning how to live and die by choice.

To the contrary, being hard on yourself is an intention of discipline with a negative reinforcement.

Expect Nothing

Life's greatest disappointments come from not getting what we expected. High expectations result in high levels of disappointment, exhaustion and disillusionment. To expect something, is to believe that you don't currently have it, but that it is possible to get it. In order to have it, you do all that is required of you and then sit back and wait for it to happen. However, you have no control over the outside factors that also play a part. Expectations are a dangerous thing.

> --They require investment.
> --They depend on external factors.
> --They are often filled with attachment.
> --They are mostly head-level expectations.
> --Expectations activate the ego.
> --Judgement is required in the world of expectations.
> --Most importantly, what you expect may not be what you need.

If you have made your dream into your way of life, you will not need to invest any time or energy on expectations. All that you need and desire will be drawn to you before you even know you need it.

Take a long look at what I have just said:

....If you have made your dream into your way of life....

This is all you need to know in order to achieve everything that you can imagine for yourself. Don't waste time with expectations.

104

Simply identify what your life needs to be like in order to make the dream your way of life, and then start living it. Forget about the external factors; it is your inner world that draws it to you or takes you farther away.

Keeping Up With the Jones'

A sure way to kill all possibility of having peace in your life and enjoying the success of your dreams, is to get caught up in the game of keeping up with the Jones'. Never mind what they are doing, what they have, how they are, how they are not, and so on. In order for you to know your own life and achieve your goals, your attention needs to be firmly set on your reality and no one else's. If you spend your life trying to keep up with family members, neighbors, or acquaintances, you will wake up one day to realize that you have everything that they wanted, but very little, if anything, of what you wanted. Your life will be their dream and not your own. I am continually amazed at the amount of people who are going through this process, and not even noticed that they were on this path. It is understandable that it is very easy to get caught up in society's game. Many get focused on achieving validation, affirmation and love from external sources. I have done it, I am sure that you have done it, and there is no doubt that, at some point in life, everyone will spend some time lost in the madness of that reality.

Take back the power you have always had, and stay alert in relation to what is happening in your life. What is going on in anyone else's life is none of your business. Here are a few insights into the Jones':

105

--They are not all that happy.

--They don't really care about you.

--When they say you are looking lovely, your house is beautiful, and your new car is fantastic, they are lying. In fact, they probably loathe the fact that you have imitated them.

--They don't have the happy family they portray to the world.

--Mrs. Jones is not very impressed with her children's exam results, even though she boasts about them to you. This is likely because she is never happy with anything.

--The Jones' spend most of their year, trying to pay off the installments on their credit card from last year's big holiday. You know, the one that made your face fall when you heard about it, and caused you to think 'how come I can't have a holiday like that?'

--They think that YOU are the Jones' and are only doing what they are doing in order to impress you. How is that for competition?

--They think you have everything.

--They think your life is perfect.

--They think you have it all worked out.

--They want your validation, affirmation and appreciation.

--They are stuck in a game unknown to themselves, and they want out too.

Don't ever lose sight of the fact that nothing is what it seems, even if you have looked into it, think you have figured it out, and you now 'know' exactly what is going on.... NO, you don't. It is sad but true, unless it's not, that we don't yet know how to celebrate life with and for each other. Part of your responsibility in life is to learn how to celebrate your world with all of the glory you can muster up. From this place you will be able to build real, sincere and heart-level relationships with the Jones' and everyone else. Get focused, get loving, and get inside yourself.

The Wisdom of Experience

There is no doubt that the life you have already lived is the greatest gift you have in creating the change you now want. However, so many people continue down the road of life and never realize that all they need, they have from experience alone. It doesn't matter what age you are, although the older you are, the more likely it is that your pool of experiences will be deeper and richer in terms of your previous experience. All you need to do is take time out of your busy life to reflect over the events of the past, and see what those moments have given you. Every moment has given you something. Sit in a quiet place with your eyes closed.....

1. Remember the last time you felt the feeling you are feeling in this moment.
2. Revisit the last time you felt this way in detail. Observe the entire experience and answer the following question: What is needed in this situation in order to give me what I really need?
3. Trust the answer you hear and then open your eyes and apply that answer to your current situation.

This is not an invitation to live in the past. It is simply an exercise that you can do to learn how to create a better now. You glance back, in order to learn from the experiences you have already had. Of course, you can skip this and repeat the pattern, recreate the experience, and suffer the consequences again, but *why would you want to do that?*

It may take a few attempts to get this working in your life in such a way that it is effective and worth practicing. The answer you get will need to be tailored to your current situation, but many times, there is no tailoring required. Within you, there are unlimited resources of wisdom and answers to all of your life's questions. You simply need to learn different ways to access these resources. It is best to create your own ways of getting the answers, and it is often more beneficial to do this, as other people's ways of accessing their inner wisdom may not work for you. If you follow your own inner guidance, you will have a lot more success. It is best to create your own tools and systems for self-discovery.

The Old Folks Home

In my late teen years, I was struggling internally with something that had happened in my life a few years previously. I wasn't fully clear on what was happening, or why it was happening, but I was very clear in knowing that I needed to believe that life was worth living. I needed hope, insight and information; but God didn't seem to be talking much to me, although I looked very hard to find him.

I was working at a part-time job in the local hospital, and every so often, would be stationed in what I referred to as the 'old folks ward'. This was the geriatric wing of the hospital. In reality, the people who lived there were there to die with as much peace and dignity as possible. Many of them needed 24-hour care and their families needed help. At the time, this hospital seemed to be the answer. I wouldn't be a supporter of such places today, but back then, I was thinking with a relatively society-oriented mind.

One day, while shaving and cleaning some of the older men, I got to thinking that they had lived a long time. They had a lot of experience that I didn't have, and most likely had plenty of wisdom that they might be willing to share. Perhaps they could remember the highs and lows of life, and what is worth doing and what is not. With that stream of thinking, I began my visits and that day, I spent time with more than a dozen male residents, all of whom were in their last years, and some of whom were in their last months or weeks. I asked them all one simple question:

'What advice would you have for a young lad like me, as I set out in life?'

The discussions I had were amazing. These men had experienced life in a way that I never had, and in many cases, I would never want to have. We spoke about their families, their losses, their hopes and dreams, their sadness, their disappointments and the paths life's journey took them down. Some of these were conscious choices, and others were forced upon them (or so it seemed to them). We spoke of the women they loved, some that they lost, and the children they watched grow up.

Essentially, all of the conversations were very sad, and the way these seasoned and honorable men were ending their lives was just as sad. Even though we laughed about things they would say, most of them acknowledged that there were too many unanswered questions for them to have peace, and death was something they feared. I have no doubt that many of them hung on to life and died long and difficult deaths, simply because they were afraid to let go and move on.

Imagine being so afraid, so out of your own life and your own sense of self, that you feared death to the point of choosing to die slowly, painfully and alone. What have we done to this world and to our brothers and sisters?

The following are the highlights of the advice my older brothers gave me, as I was beginning my own life's journey:

>--'Don't take life too seriously, son; you will only end up disappointed, annoyed, tired, and lost.'

>--'Don't worry about money; if you give it too much attention it will own you and the truth is, it's worthless anyway.'

>--'Travel everywhere you can, whenever you can.'

--'Think hard before you have children; they are fantastic but they come with a high price on your pocket, your mind, your faith, your sanity and your dream of a quiet life. They also arrive home one day with young ones of their own and you have to start all over again.'

--'Fall in love with someone who wants you to succeed and shares your dreams.'

--'Move slowly, and don't think that achieving great things makes you a great man.'

--'Take some time to actually answer some of the questions you ask yourself.'

--'Laugh as often as possible.'

--'Don't put trust in anything other than yourself.'

--'Don't stop believing in yourself.'

--'Don't be afraid to take risks.'

--'Do the best you can.'

--'Don't bother saving for a rainy day. If you do that, you will be making a choice not to bother living on the days you're saving.'

--'Stop asking stupid questions, son, and get on with shaving me!'

You don't want to get to your death bed, alone, sad and full of knowing, but without the experiences you dreamed of.

The Meaning of Success

You will succeed or fail depending on the understanding you have of the concept of success. Do you know what success means to you, and if so, are you living congruently with that meaning? Is success more to do with things outside of you or things within you?

You can have it all, and you can achieve success on every front. The most important thing is to prioritize it so that you take on the challenge of change from a perspective that is going to get you where you want to be. Otherwise, you will be wandering around, bumping into small successes and failures, in the hope that at some point in time, you will stumble into the dream and have abundance in mind, heart and pocket.

Success is not any one definition. You define what success is for you, and then you realize that you have it already. There is no big mystery to figure out. Life is simply a process of birth and death for you to access in such a way, that you live from choice, free will, compassion, and love. This is all done from a consciousness of peace.

What is success for you? Once this is answered you'll know the direction in which you must travel.

Are You an Actor or a Re-actor?

Many people go through life reacting to what they have been told is right or wrong, true or false, good or bad. They live in the context of someone else's concept of life and living, and while stuck in that prison, they think they are free.

In some cases there are people who believe they are free to the point that they die fighting to defend that freedom. Think about it this way. Scott is a 22-year-old soldier in Afghanistan and he went there after joining the army because he believed that we are free, and that freedom should be protected. He is lead to believe that he is free to the point that he will choose to die. However, once there, he realizes that all is not what it seems, and he decides that this is not the right thing for him anymore. But to leave, he has only three options:

1. Get shot. Freedom?
2. Go to jail for refusing to engage any further. Freedom?
3. Serve his time and do his 'tour of duty'. Freedom?

When you react and engage with other people's rules and regulations, you give those people jurisdiction over you, which is giving them power over you. Once they have power, you will spend your life reacting to them, their wishes, their rules and their demands. This is not the way to create change, achieve freedom, and live according to your dreams. In fact, it is living as a 're-actor'.

What **you** want requires you to go against the grain, step out of the boat and walk on the water, and be in your own power, 100%. To live as an 'actor' is to make a choice to live according to your own rules and regulations. In relation to others, you simply need to know that you will harm no one else, take nothing that is not yours, and do all you can to live consciously and from a place of love.

It is not an easy road in the traditional sense of the word. That is, until you actually get to the point where you are fully present in your way of being at an emotional, psychological and mindful level. That means that you are there fully and without doubt, question or concern, and you live from confidence and an inner strength that nothing can shake or threaten. Remember, it is about 'experiencing' the growth, not getting there.

You are Success Waiting to Happen
What do you believe is keeping you from your dreams at this stage? You are the very success that you seek. It is not something that you get from the outside world; it comes with no validation, no appreciation and no external offerings.

Imagine that you have just found an orphaned eagle on the side of the road; he is sad and upset. You stop and ask, 'Why are you sad?', and the eagle says, 'I dream of being an eagle'. You quickly realize that he doesn't know he is an eagle, and you are filled with excitement because you are going to give him the best news ever. You then tell him, 'But you *are* an eagle'. Not knowing that he is an eagle and never having any one to teach him that he is an eagle, he doesn't believe you, and continues to cry and sit there, still dreaming of being an eagle.

What do you do now?

What is your next move?

If the eagle is not willing to trust you, you cannot make him believe. What ideas can you come up with to help the eagle to believe that he is an eagle?

Now take those ideas and apply them to your life. You are success and you are waiting to happen; meaning that you just need to see and believe in your true nature. You will realize that you already have all that you dream of; you are the change and the abundance.

Do you realize that everything is a perception and everything is dependent on your ability to see it? Creation happens by your observation of it. What you focus on becomes your reality. What is it you want? What will it take to make it happen? Now do it.

Engaging In 'the process' of finding the success in your 'failures':

1. List all the moments in your life that you judge as 'failures'.

2. After each item on the list write out what that moment, situation or circumstance taught you (each one will have taught you something, so look for the lesson.)

3. Identify what you have in your life because of it.

4. Write out the list of 'failures' again, but this time re-title them in a positive way and title the list, 'My most precious moments'.

5. Take some time to realize that life is all about perception, and if you allow yourself to see things in a new light, they will be different in reality.

Contradiction # 7

What's Hard Is Easy

1. How do I perceive life?
2. How does my perception of life fit into what I am experiencing?
3. Is my perception of life holding me back or moving me forward?
4. What are the values that I believe are non-negotiable according to my perception of life?
5. How much of my perception of life is truly mine and without influence from others?

Another way to explain what is meant by perception is to use the language of 'image', 'picture' or 'movie'. In doing so, the question shifts from, 'What is my perception?' to, 'What is the picture I have created that tells me what I can do, what I can achieve, what is available to me or what is not?' What are the movies I play in my head that show me what can or cannot be achieved? What is the image I reference within my mind when asking if I can or cannot?

The only limits in your life are the limits that are placed there by you. As you paint the picture of your life as you would like it to be, the only limits and obstacles that will exist are the limits and obstacles that you paint into the picture. Even if you are struggling with a certain element of your life, or a problem that has arisen for you, the solution is there. The solution is a lot closer than you think.

'The Map is Not the Territory'

The map of life you have as your reference guide is far smaller than the total territory that exists for you to travel and learn about. If you have ever had a road map in your car that is folded into many folds in order to store it away, you will understand that on the flip side of each fold there are more roads (territory) for you to explore. When you open the map to find a specific route to your destination, you do not stop searching simply because you have come to the edge of the page. You turn the page and continue to follow the road. Along the way you may come across villages, towns and cities that you have never been to before, but you don't question the need to drive through them to get to your destination; so it is with life.

There are many new places that exist outside the boundaries of the map you have been referencing, and these are essential places to move through in search of your outcome. If you stick to only one page of your map, in other words, if you see life as existing in its totality within the boundaries of your experience, you will never experience anything new. In this case, what do you do if your destination exists outside of your map? The call from the spirit within is always one to travel to new destinations and to move outside of what is familiar to you.

118

By traveling through the new territory, you will face new issues and new challenges. You will find new things to celebrate. This means you will have the opportunity to flex emotional, psychological, physical and spiritual muscles that you may not have known existed. However, without taking the time to choose this new path and to accept that life exists beyond your perception and understanding, you will run the risk of remaining a person of limited experience, with a limited share of life's wealth.

The phrase, 'the map is not the territory', is telling you that you do not know everything, even if you like to think you do. It is inviting you to know that other people and new experiences hold a wealth of information and knowledge that you do not yet have. Without these new challenges, you will continue to fall short of your dreams.

As you go into uncharted territory along your journey, you will:

--learn more about yourself
--discover what matters most
--see both your weaknesses and your strengths
--find out how to celebrate in a new way
--be forced to pick yourself up, and keep going after you have fallen (maybe many times)
--explore and become familiar with the new experiences of life, before you once again go beyond the newer territory, and reach further into the next step beyond

This map and the new territory that is being referred to includes the world *around* you in terms of relationships, jobs, friends, money, social life and hobbies. Even more importantly, it refers to the map and territory that exists *within* you.

It is an invitation for you to take a moment and realize that you know very little about yourself. A much larger world within and beyond, is waiting to be discovered. There is so much about who you really are, that you are not yet aware of, much less understand. By not seizing the opportunity to explore the new territory, you are not getting to know yourself. It is with this in mind, that it can confidently be said that *you* are the only real barrier to manifesting all you desire in your life.

Of course, your perception of life and your willingness to see this as true or false, will determine the greatness of the picture you paint and the greatness of the experience you have. In saying you know yourself, you are living within the bounds of certainty, and your life experiences will reflect only those limits.

Aren't you at least a little curious to discover the person that you really are? The undiscovered you is the one who can make magic happen; it is the you that attracts wealth, well-being, joy, bliss, and the forces of the universe to work in your favor. In addition, the undiscovered you is the one who holds the solutions to what you currently percieve to be your problems. It is simply a case of having limited information and living *with* that, versus remaining open to all information and living *from* that.

Living *with* what you know puts your capacity to comprehend and understand in charge of your experiences. Living *from* a place and space of all-knowing puts the universe in charge, and when the universe is in charge, all things are available to you. All you need be concerned with is being in charge of your reactions and choices. Be sure you are aware of the differences between actions and reactions. That is in relation to what the universe places in your path. The difference is as vast as the universe is wide.

We spend so much of our lives considering things and forming opinions based on how we feel, what our understanding of a situation is, and with the idea of how the outcome might affect us, others, or the world. We decide what our contribution to that person, place or thing will be, based on these internal deliberations. The problem with this is quite obvious. We are continuously making decisions, filtering information and drawing conclusions with the same pattern we have always used. Obviously, using the same formula in an attempt to create something new, does not work.

Many wise teachers and mentors have said in various forms, 'If you always do what you have always done, you will always get what you have always gotten'. In order to make changes, there must be a significant 'awakening'. There must be a moment when the entire world, as you know it, shifts and begins to show you a new set of options, a new way, and possibilities with practical elements that you have not yet thought of. In order for this awakening to happen, you need to jump off the edge of old beliefs within the self, the very ones you have taken refuge in for so long.

There must be a realization that some of the alledged 'truths' of life, the fundamental foundations upon which life has been built, are in fact, false.

In order to move forward, it is important to question your beliefs and challenge your own perspective of life and the world. Don't be afraid to allow yourself to find the flaws in some of the things you thought you knew to be right. There you will find great learning and great reason; reason to know and reason to grow.

Forcing Change

Trying to force the necessary change to happen in your life is about as wise as trying to push water up a hill, or trying to change the course of a river with a soup spoon. Change cannot be made to happen; it is simply *allowed* to happen. To put it more accurately, there is nothing you can do to prevent change. Where you want to get to, is the same place life wants you to get to. You are on the same side, fighting the same fight and moving with the same intention. However, knowing how to dance with life is the key to your happiness. There are things you do, and things you don't do, when you're seeking change.

There is no way around the fact that you are the person in the picture, and the life you are living is your life, your responsibility. When discussing what to do in order to allow change to happen, close to the top of the list is to 'accept' this responsibility. Fully accept it, don't partially accept it. You need to be 100% committed to knowing that your life is your full responsibility. That also means accepting responsibility for 'what not to do';

learn to stop blaming other things, people and other situations for your current issues. Yes, there have been influencing factors in the past, but this moment is this moment, and it really has little, if anything, to do with your past.

In accepting responsibility for your life right now, you are also accepting responsibility to move forward. The future world that you experience has its foundations established in the now. Dream the dream of what you want your life to be like and then, using the wisdom of your experience, identify all that you need to do to achieve this dream. In doing so, you need to allow the change to happen around you, with you, and in spite of you. This means learning to do what you need to do, but letting go of your need to control the experience, so that you allow each day to bring you whatever it will. It means being careful not to judge anyone you meet, anything you see, or any experiences that you are confronted with in any given day.

When you are working for change in your life you have a contract with life itself that is between the both of you. The outcome will be reached and achieved, if you have the wisdom to know when to do nothing, go with the flow and enjoy the journey. It may be more difficult than you would expect, but it is one of the most important things to learn.

There is a force of life that connects all, knows all, and is all. Life does not need you to teach it; you need to be open to learn from it. This invitation is one that opens a door to a magical experience and creates magical moments. When you let go of the need to be right, and let go of the fear of being hurt, all of the love of life will come to rest within you. It is from this place that you will be fueled, encouraged, loved, honored, and valued. You will be free to be true to your own individual dharma (your essential quality of character) and purpose. Then and only then, will you truly understand the meaning behind the truth that, 'you are the teacher and the student', and there is no other but you. You will then grasp the understanding that you have within you all wisdom, but it can only be discovered when you become empty of all knowledge. You will know your greatness; you will know you are God; and there is no other. Simply learn to sit in silence, and all that is essential and necessary will come to you. From that moment, take action and have the courage to work with life as your partner. Seeing yourself as separate from life will simply disconnect the singer from the song, and the change you long for will continue to remain at a distance.

Feeling the Flow

If you have ever visited a doctor or hospital and had a nurse check your pulse, you know that they are checking to ensure that the rate at which your heart is beating is balanced and healthy. A pulse rate that is too slow or too fast often causes alarm, as it can suggest that something is not going according to plan, and the result could be fatal. The nurse doesn't need to ask you anything in order to get the information she needs. The experience of taking the pulse is enough to give her the insight she is seeking.

Life has a pulse. It has an energy flow, a vibration, a resonance. If you can tap into this, you will quite easily download all the information, knowledge and wisdom you need to create a shift in your life's journey. The promise of tapping into the flow is not a promise of an easy life, at least not initially. Gradually, life does get easier; when you are tapped into the universal pulse, you are indeed saying 'yes' to the law of least effort. You are allowing life, and the silence of life, to do all of the heavy duty work. Life gets easier, and the things you need the most, find their way to you with a seemingly effortless ease.

In the initial stages, however, the shift that occurs can be overwhelming, and can bring great challenge, as well as great liberation. If we are being in the present moment and allowing all things to be what they are without judgment or labeling, the result will be one that empowers and liberates us.

It is worth noting that the response you choose to engage in at this stage of your journey (or any stage in the journey), will determine the outcome. You are the master of your reality and your perception of reality can produce the blocks that are creating your destiny.

Tapping into this pulse of life, this life force that seems to exist all around us, within us, and beyond this time and space is not always as easy as we may think or are lead to believe.
It is difficult because it means learning how to speak a different language, and learning how to walk a different walk. The new language is the language of life, the language of God. It is without words and without context; it is the language of feeling, the

language of love, the language of acceptance. It is the language of the heart.

There is little logic attached to this pulse. You will find it when you are sitting with your eyes closed and your mind silenced. It resonates with a beautiful sound; but the sound is heard with something other than your ears. It is heard at the very depths of your being. It brings with it a feeling of peace, a sense of joy and a confidence that reaches far beyond what the mind can comprehend. You'll know it when you have found it, because you have thoughts without thinking; you see without your eyes; feel without any touch; and rest without effort. In this place, there is an answer to all your questions, and a powerful question with each answer.

It is here that you begin to explore the connections of life that you have only tried to imagine. There is no scientist, sage, priest or philosopher that can put into words the experiences that await you in this place. The pulse of life is the breath of all that has ever been, all that is, and all that ever will be. It is that place where nothing is required and everything is available. While sitting in the pulse of life, you are resting in the deepest part of who you are. It is beyond material things, and is not bothered by the issues of the mind. This state of being is removed from the world that you experience in your average day, and goes ever deeper into itself in a spiraling dance that brings you to bliss. It is you; you are the pulse of life and the pulse exists for you, because of you and as you.

From this place you have access to all you have dreamed of. You have love, compassion and peace. The things of your life that were once troubles and worries evaporate and are replaced with a gentle forgiveness. Your heart becomes alive in the most profound way, and your spirit speaks to you with the voice and authority of God. In this place you are home, and you have entered the creative breath of life.

Dancing with Fear

It is only your fear that will keep you from this experience of the self. When you are in fear, of fear, or with fear, you are moving in a direction that is opposite to the direction where you discover what you were born to find. The challenge is to learn to dance 'with' the fear. Don't worry about trying to get rid of it. It is a part of life, and without it you would likely be prevented from finding the flow of life and living in the wisdom of the self. Fear is there for a reason, and on occasion, you may even feel flooded with different reasons to be afraid. The reasons are not all that important. Fear is a natural part of life, just like the experience of love and the experience of excitement. Do you try to find a solution to love or excitement when they come your way? Most likely not; it's a safe bet that you kick the door open and say, 'I'll have more of that, thank you'. So it is with fear, as with any other experience in life.

Do not try to push it away, because the more you resist it, the more it will persist. Instead, kick open the door and invite it in. What is the point of trying to avoid it? It will remain until you finally face it at some point. It is to your advantage to do it now, and learn all you can from it.

The invitation that is delivered to your reality by fear is an invitation to learn how to dance. Yes, you read it right; you need to learn how to dance the tango with fear. It is a raw and passionate dance with many moves. However, unless you learn the dance, you will continue to step on each others toes. Imagine a pair of dancers stepping on each other's toes throughout an entire song, and you will soon see the discomfort and the pain that can result; never mind the challenge of knowing they have to dance together again, and again, and again. The obvious thinking would be, 'I need to find a new dance partner' or 'I'm out of here', as you hide around the corner, hoping to remain in the shadow until a chance comes for you to make a hasty retreat. Learning the dance is the easiest option, especially when you consider a life of having your toes stomped on, and fear has very big feet. Besides, you don't have the option of finding a new partner. The fact is, that learning to dance with fear is learning to dance with the self.

Fear is something that exists within, you cannot avoid it. For instance, trying to avoid it would be the same as trying to get through life without ever spending any time with yourself; it can't be done. Although many have tried, none have succeeded. Those who try to ignore or escape fear are easy to find; they're in the bar; in the casinos, taking drugs, having affairs, and beeping their horns at the world as it pulls out in front of them; or they are telling everybody else how to live. Some even move many miles from their old life in the hope that a new life will solve the problem, only to discover soon after the move that fear lives there too. Therefore, it is obvious, we all need to learn the dance.

By 'dance' I mean that you need to learn how to move with the fear, and not against it. Sit with each feeling and see what it brings up for you. What are the memories, the pain, the images, the colors, the sounds, and the thoughts? How does this fear affect your body? Where do you feel the fear, and what does that feeling cause within you? It may not be easy to see when fear has a grip on you, but the very thing you need most in the moment you are feeling the fear is to surrender to it, by going into it, and see what message it is bringing you. Have you ever heard the saying "Keep your friends close, but your enemies closer"? This applies to fear and learning to dance with it. Unless you find out how fear moves, what motivates it, and what gift it is trying to bring you, you will simply continue to step on each other's toes.

Dancing with fear also requires that you put yourself first; it requires that you take the time to go within; it demands that you put a hold on getting involved in other people's dramas; and it asks that you learn how to navigate the inner world with all its dark shadows and lonely crevices. It is certainly one of life's great contradictions, but learning this dance, and allowing yourself to explore the loneliness with all its dark spaces, is the very thing that will bring the light back into your life. When the lights are on you will be able to see what is really there and you will soon discover that the future does not have to be a lonely one.

Of course, you could take the fast train by putting the fear down to an illusion. That is something you have created with the conditioning the world has taught you. By seeing that it is simply an illusion within your own psyche, you will be able to laugh at it, and then put your mind, your attention and your actions on those things that are not illusions. You will no longer harbor the illusion that you will be burned by its flame. Of course, many of us need the illusion, and don't want to allow ourselves to believe that beating it can be as easy as choosing to see it as the illusion it is, and nothing more. Remember, when life seems too hard, 'It's only an illusion', as is the pain it causes, the anxiety it creates, and the self-sabotage that is most certainly going to come from the pain and the anxiety of the fear. After all, what you resist persists!

All Things are Connected

Everything in the world is connected to everything else in the world, therefore, we are all one with everything, and each other. Our past is connected to our present and our present is connected to our future. Every breath we have taken is connected to every other breath that has ever come into or left our body. The people on the street that we have not yet met are part of our life and the people at the polar ends of the earth are also connected to us. The dreams we have fantasized about, are connected to the dreams we haven't even created yet. The words we have spoken throughout our entire life are connected to the experiences we will create ten years from now. The prayers we have prayed and the hopes we have held on to are all connected to the joys and the pain we have felt and lived through in our life. Each person that has passed from our world is connected to those yet to grace us with their presence. Just as the moon is connected to the sea and the sun is connected to the forest of trees, we are connected to all aspects of life. Each part of our body is connected to every other part of our body, and enables it to do its job. Our thoughts are connected to our behavior in the same way that the bird is connected to the sky. Our feelings are connected to our experiences, as the thorns are connected to the rose bush.

There is truly nowhere to hide from the self or from the 'Source.' Separation is the ultimate illusion. To believe that there is separation, that we can have an experience without it having an impact on all other experiences, is as foolish as saying that a child can be born without a mother. Everything we do, everything we say, every feeling we entertain, every thought we play with, every move we make, every tear we shed, and every smile we share with the world is connected to who we are now, and who we will become in the future. There is no escape from the fact that we are one with the world, and therefore, connected in the most dramatic manner. Our thoughts today have a direct effect on the world around us, both seen and unseen; so it is that separation is an illusion.

Within us there is wisdom in relation to this fact. Our lives are a journey of uncovering the truths that will lead us to a resting place within ourselves. It allows us to know and feel this connection. The separation we think we experience is simply a trick of the eye, and a trick of the mind. Our socialization, religions, and life experiences may suggest that we are separate, but even they are connected to the unified field of oneness. As we cannot separate the sun from its rays, the singer from the song, nor can we be separated from ourselves. The world around us is simply a reflection of all the aspects and elements of who we are.

When we look outside of ourselves, we are simply seeing that which is within us and when we look within, we are learning the truth of that which exists in the world around us. Of course, we have many choices in relation to all things at all times. In choosing to ignore the interconnectedness of all things, we are closing the door to discovering the true nature of life and ourselves. This creates and reinforces the illusion that is separation. Living in the illusion will only bring with it, things of the illusion. It is time to get out of the illusion and into the self. To understand this concept, we must let go of the thoughts and rely on the most powerful sense of all, our inner experiences. Trust those gut feelings that we call our instincts, as they are the whispers from our very essence, and the authentic self that knows the truth.

The anger we feel at the person who recently offended us, is connected to the hurt that we felt or experienced in our life many years ago. It is in the very same way that the love we feel for your partner is connected to the smile our mother offered us the moment we were born. Much of our pain and hurt in life comes from our living from the belief that 'separation is real'. Those things we label as hurt, pain, depression, or anxiety, are only the cries of our spirit as it tries to let us know that we cannot leave any part of ourselves in the past. We must live in the present.

The greatest challenge that most people face is learning how to live in the now and integrate into the present moment all of who we are, the whole person, including the *you* that was (past) and the *you* that will be (future). The true journey of life is a journey back to the self. It is a journey of seeing, believing and living from the connectedness of all things, and of being responsible for our own reality. This means we are responsible for creating our own reality, positive or negative.

As hard as it is to grasp the concept that we choose our feelings at all times, it is true. We are the ones who make the choice to feel hurt, depression, or to feel powerlessness. To blame another person, situation or thing for our disempowerment, is to play with the illusion of separation. There is no doubt that other people can have an effect on us in life, but ultimately, we are each responsible for what we choose to do with that reality. It is not unfair to say that those who cause us pain can be the greatest gifts in our lives. They are here to teach us great lessons through experiences. It requires that we allow ourselves to go within in order to see how their actions or words are challenging us. It is a reminder to connect with the power that is untapped and waiting to be released. These situations can be seen as reasons to connect at a deeper level so we are not so vulnerable in the future to outside influences.

It is only when you are not living the connection with the self, that an external factor can cause pain or harm. Our pain in life is as much our choosing as is our healing. Think about it; when what we percieve as pain is done unto us, it is we who choose to hold

133

onto it or let it pass. That is true no matter how great the pain may seem. It is because we are connected to all things, all solutions, and all aspects of the experience. It's a tough pill to swallow, but it is a lot easier to take the spoon of medicine than to live with the consequences of the illusion.

For Flux Sake

Change is always happening and you have two choices: go with it or resist it. Either way, change is still going to happen. The easier option is to go with it but, of course, if you like the hardship and the drama you can always say 'no'. Change is not something to be afraid of, nor is it bad thing. Just like resistance, turning your back on change is like trying to swim upstream against the full flow of the downstream current. It is like trying to stop a leaking boat by sticking your finger in the hole. Yes, you might make some progress, but soon you will be exhausted from the effort required. The forces of nature always come out ahead. Nature holds the highest hand in the deck.

It is the old 'better the devil you know, than the one you don't' thinking, that causes most of the resistance to change. By not allowing for change to be a factor in your life, you are not allowing for the possibility, and the potentiality, that change will bring into it.

Change is a wonderful thing when you learn how to go with it, but it is excruciatingly painful when you don't. Resistance to change will play havoc with your balance and bring more discomfort than almost anything else in life. Why is this so?

134

Because, you spend your time worrying, planning, preparing, living in fear and resisting it, when it is going to happen anyway. Consider all that energy, all those sleepless nights, all that preoccupation, all those lost hours of daylight sitting in a darkened room, hiding from the world of change, when it will happen anyway; you still have to manage the consequences. Only this time, it is worse because your energy levels are down; you're feeling the effects of the anxiety; you're in another mental argument with the world; and you just don't seem to have any more of the creativity or desire to learn how to negotiate with the new life situation. 'You're goosed' (as we say in Ireland), 'you're shagged' (as they say in England), 'you're kyboshed' (as they say in.... somewhere), and you're finished (as you say in YOUR HEAD)!

If you are resisting change, chances are that you are still trying to catch up with yourself after the last change, and the one before that. Give up the fight and the self-defeating sabotage; learn to let go and let change happen. It is inevitable, so why resist?

For most people, the resistance is all about the fear of something happening that they can't handle and that something will leave them lost, confused, tired, goosed, shagged, kyboshed, finished! Are you getting the message? You are creating the very thing you are trying to avoid by resisting the change.

Watch life in the cycle of one year. We go from one season into the next. That is nature (the greatest teacher of life) showing us that change must happen in order for life to continue. Life and death are two sides of the same coin. The purpose of life is to learn to die. The ultimate fear of change is the fear of death, the unknown. We are afraid of letting go; letting go of our life as we know it. However, without the capacity to let go, we will have our hands full of the same stuff for our entire life. That is unless or until, we come to our senses and drop it all, for the easier option of being free. We need to learn to die to ourselves as we are today, in order for who we are growing into, to take its breath and live. There is a value in allowing death to happen that is so significant it brings with it the code to unlocking our true nature.

--How can you expect to get that job you have always dreamed of, if you won't let go of what you have?
--How will you ever meet Mr. or Ms. Right if you don't let go of the fear of not finding them?
--How can you ever expect to create financial freedom if you don't let the death of insecurity happen?
--How can you ever stand tall in life if you don't stop sitting down (so to speak)?
--How can you ever think of finding peace if you won't let worry and anxiety die?
--How can you change your life if you don't let the need for certainty go?

YOU CAN NOT do any of these things. It just doesn't work that way.

Change is your key to the place within you that holds all the answers. Let the change come and then, let what that change brings go, so you can allow more change. It is the only way, if you truly desire to create your own happiness. It is a contradiction, a paradox, that causes great strife for people but you need to realize that what you believe to be the easy way is actually the hardest way.

Hard and Easy are Just Judgements

'Hard' and 'Easy' are just mental judgements, so let them go too. In truth, they will get in your way. When you are living with judgements like easy and hard you are going to find that you are creating points of resistance without even knowing it. We all have certain ways of thinking about things attached to 'measurement sticks', and these two words are no different. When you see something as easy you will get excited about it and when you see something as hard you may get frustrated or anxious, even thinking about it. How difficult it is to begin something that you believe is hard? It will be *very hard*, and you will probably procrastinate. It was bad enough when it was hard, now it is *very hard,* so the chances of you giving it a go have dramatically decreased. When you think something is easy, it's likely that you will go ahead and do it without any anxiety.

It might be good for you to change the language you use in order to overcome this issue. The language you use will depend on what works best for you. Or you may decide to leave the language, but change your interpretation of the words. This may seem like game playing and silliness but the result is neither. It can be highly effective. For me, I use the same language but I change the interpretation of the words. Something that is *easy* means I can do it with no worries and no strife. The lesson learned from it will be gentle, possibly insightful, gained with confidence, and certainly enjoyable. When something is *hard* for me, it means that the lesson is most likely very important, and something that will be a great resource to me with new knowledge, skills or capacity that I can apply to other areas of my life. This results in even the 'hard' things being worth doing well, with care, with undivided attention, and with great respect.

What do you think your life would be like if you stopped judging and labeling things as easy or hard? What might you learn? The greatest example of this in my life was making the move from the secure salary of a company employee to the *'Oh my God, extremely hard world of self-employment'*. The thought of making a living without the salary, and having to depend on myself every day, knowing that I might not get paid at all some months, was daunting. I did it anyway, and guess what I discovered? I discovered that I will never be without earnings. I need only 'me' to make it happen and it keeps on happening. In fact, that hard thing is now one of the easiest things in my life. To be honest, I can now appreciate how *hard* it was to work for someone else and make them rich, as I remained in the same place doing the same thing for the same money. Mind you the 'hard' in that situation was the very thing that drove me to doing what I did.

So, perhaps what is hard is actually easy and sometimes the 'easy' road is actually the hardest. Furthermore, everything is an experience and is therefore, neither easy nor hard. Are you still with me?

It's All Just Experience

Here is another great way to look at the world and at the same time get rid of most, if not all, of your judgements. Simply look at everything as an experience, something that is valuable to you because it teaches you lessons, opens your eyes, gives you insight, creates opportunity, and allows you to discover things you have yet to uncover. Look at everything as an experience, everything. Doing the house work, an experience; driving in the country, an experience; having that tough conversation with someone, an experience; that hospital stay, an experience; the fitness workout, an experience; the job interview, an experience.

If you look at all of life like this, you are free of judgements. Therefore, you are free from the expectations that go hand in hand with the judgements. Here is a simple example:

> You get word of a job interview, and you consider it to be just an experience. In doing so, you let go of expectations. All of a sudden, you don't need to get caught up in the worry of not getting it 'right'. You don't need to let the anxiety of saying the wrong thing take over. There is no need to try to oversell yourself. If they don't like you for you, that is okay too, because now you're not taking things personally, it's just an experience. Gone are the days of endless worry about who else might be 'up for the job'... it is just an experience.

This does make life easier. You see, it's all about your perspective, which is the way you choose to see things. There is nothing more powerful than the way we think about life and what it has in store for us. Our thoughts are powerful in creating worry or freedom. This one also tackles the fear issue, the change issue, the uncertainty issue, and the 'am I good enough' issue.

You can apply the 'it's all just an experience' approach to your past also. The broken relationship, just an experience; the job that you were let go from, just an experience; the illness that hit you hard, just an experience, and on it goes. Even death is just an experience. It is neither right nor wrong, neither good nor bad, neither better nor worse, neither easy nor hard, JUST AN EXPERIENCE.

Here is another little contradiction for you. Remember to be serious about not taking life too seriously. Learn to laugh at yourself and learn to laugh at life. There is nothing as good as laughter to take the sting out of the challenges and the difficulties of life. We often meet people and situations that are hyped up with seriousness, and it is easy to get caught up in the hullabaloo. There are so many things that demand our attention every day. When you see them as nothing more than experiences, you have the choice to leave them on the 'must do' list (or the 'should do', or 'to do' list), or to knock them off for now and be happy knowing that the particular experience can wait for another day. It allows decision making to become a lot easier; it lifts the guilt; it eliminates the need, and it allows for a little 'I'm back in control'. This is a great way to make some more room in life for time to laugh, relax, do nothing (which is so important), and be at peace.

The Never-Ending Battle to Love the SelfAll of the things we have discussed so far in terms of resistance – being too serious, anxiety, fear, avoiding change, judgement and all the rest of the illusions, ('those very serious life issues') are all just ways in which we create diversions. We tend to manufacture so many things to keep us busy. As long as we are busy with these things, we do not have to be busy with what matters most, our wellbeing. We all seem to speak of the importance of being kind and giving to the self, but it is such a challenging thing to allow to happen. The irony of the whole thing is that we are going to end up in the same place regardless of what road we take, and where is that place? That place is in facing ourselves, our needs, our heart's desires, the yearning to belong, our desire to be loved, and our need for self-acceptance.

Only last week I was going to visit someone, when I came across a diversion (detour) sign on the road. The route I would normally take was closed. So, being the balanced, accepting and patient person that I am, I saw the diversion sign and ignored it! Yep, I drove right by it and straight up the road that was marked 'closed'. This was because I like to go straight to my destination whenever possible, as I have taken too many diversions in my life. Of course, only a few minutes later I came to a hole in the road so big that you could fit a jumbo jet into it, so I turned around. Driving back down the road, I discovered that the new route was 12 miles longer on small country roads, and would add at least a half hour to my trip. Time wasn't on my side on the day in question, so I undertook the journey with a frown on my face and a few choice words in the privacy of my car.

The old saying that 'your thoughts will become your reality' being true, and me being a little forgetful sometimes, my few choice words and my not-so-cheery attitude took over. All of a sudden I was having an internal war with everyone in my life who ever caused me to frown. Finally I arrived but not in a great mood. The diversion, which was only a diversion, was my excuse that day to let go of what matters most, and engage in resistance to love myself. There were several consequesnce of my unfortunate choices that day. I missed the joy of the unexpected drive in the country; I exhausted myself emotionally and psychologically; and I am sure I wasn't the most pleasant visitor for my friend!

If you do discover that you have to take a diversions, remember what matters most, and don't forget that it's just an experience. The most important thing is to love yourself on the journey and, when you meet a diversion, love yourself a little bit more, and keep going. You will eventually find that not only was there a reason, but that even a diversion is an opportunity for growth.

We spend so much time and energy trying to get others to love us, not realizing that it's not possible for someone to love you, until you love yourself. It's not unusual for people to even lose those who love them, simply because they do not love themselves. How can you expect to appreciate someone else's love for you, when you don't even appreciate or love yourself? I mentioned earlier that the purpose of life was to learn how to die. You are living your dying right now. When you can love yourself, you will be able to allow death to happen (death of a life situation or circumstance or even physical death). However, when you cannot love yourself you will fight any and every kind of death when it calls to you. The death is inevitable, because that is what life is all about. But loving yourself allows it to be nothing more than an experience. The alternative can be long, slow, painful, empty, lonely, and filled with crippling fear.

Love yourself, you are definitely worth it. In this context, what I mean by love is simple to explain. It means acceptance that you and your life are perfect right now in this moment, regardless of what you might think, or what you might see. Don't forget that what you think and what you see, are simply the illusions you have created to avoid facing the self. Just because you have not yet been loved, or have not learned what it means to be loved, doesn't mean you have to join the party and hold out on yourself. Start now. A smile from you to you is good enough. That will lead you to another smile, and before you know it, you will be feeling the love.

Engaging In 'the process' of making what is hard easy

1. Write out a list of all the changes you want in your life that you think are simply too difficult to achieve.
2. Identify the reason for them being so hard for you to achieve.

143

3. Write out all the ways it could be achieved (do not let fear, failure, or money problems, prevent you from writing anything down).
4. Find one of the items listed in the answer to number three that feels close enough to possible.
5. Identify what part of that you could achieve and what part of it you feel you cannot achieve.
6. Identify what support system (or persons) you would need to plug into, to make the part you feel you cannot achieve possible.
7. Write out the action you need to take in relation to what you can achieve; then plug into the support system required for the rest of that change to happen.

Contradiction # 8

Death Creates Life

Although it is fair to say that very few of us have studied enough to understand the true fundamentals of this thing we call 'death', I believe it is more accurate to say that very few of us have 'lived enough' to understand this thing we call death. We are often brought up to understand that death is something that happens and there is little that anyone knows about it, and even less that we can do about it. However, this is not the case. Death is available to us to understand just as much as life. It is as accessible as anything in life that offers us understanding, exploration, and allowing. This is true unless you are not aware of it; then it will not be true for you. In which case, we can say it is true, unless it is not. That means your life will simply be a consequence of what you do not know, instead of what it is that you do know.

Learning about life and death is the beginning of an authentic journey of knowing and being, and in accepting authenticity as a way of life. We are all asked to realize that nothing is as it seems, and everything is what we make it. The journey of life is as much about death as it is about life. In truth there is nothing born without death and nothing dies without birth. These two realities are very much a part of each other, they accompany each other on every step of the road we call our journey. Understanding them, what they mean, why they are so, and what they represent, is essential to creating a balanced life of love, acceptance, peace and allowing. Without these things life can be a struggle, and once there is a struggle, there is a resistance to allowing life to be.

Death Happens Many Times

In a western society, many people believe that death is a physical existence that happens once in your life and there is little you can do about it. However, this is not the whole truth. Death happens many times when we allow it, as you will see in further discussion. In fact, death happens many times whether we allow it or not. In allowing and acknowledging it, things make a lot more sense, and life becomes less fear-filled. Furthermore, it is through allowing death that life happens. The physical death that we are all brought up to fear so much is only one element of the death that life confronts us with. What about the spiritual death, the emotional death, and the psychological death that we are all asked to embrace, and not just once in our life, but many times.

When we begin to grasp this idea and experience of consciousness, we will soon realize that death is something that comes to visit often, and for some, on a daily basis. Today we may be asked to die to who we think we are in order for the true nature of the self to show up. Some examples, we may be asked to:

--Die to our 'idea' of saving a relationship.
--Die to our understanding of faith, God and church.
--Face the death of our financial security.

146

--Be confronted with the death and passing of our plans for the future.
--Go through the death of our ideas and visions.
--Experience the death of what we once believed was our family.
--Allow death to happen in relation to what we believe is right and wrong, or good or bad.

All these deaths, and many more, are the very moments of life in which the old passes away and leaves room for the new. They are moments of growth, evolution and connection with the bigger picture of what life is really all about.

Every death, even our physical death, is simply a part of the road we are on at that current moment, yet we seem to get stuck in thinking that death is the end, death means 'no more', and death is dark and cold. This could not be further from the truth. Because all of life is a cycle, it is actually a rebirth. Death is the letting go, the beginning of the renewal, the passing on, the essential piece of life without which, life would not and could not be. To try to live life without allowing death, would be like trying to fly an airplane without wings, it simply cannot be done. The wings are essential to the flight and the science of flight relies on the wings to create the lift; if there is no lift there is no flight. So it is with life and death. Our daily deaths are the wings that allow us to fly, they allow us to move from one place to the next, they empower us to learn, see and understand. The death that this day brings, holds within it the clearance to releasing whatever it is that holds us on the runway of life, unable to lift off. Without it, we simply remain as we have always been.

Two Sides of the One Coin

Life and death are two sides of one coin. Each brings an equal amount of what is needed to us in order for us to fully know ourselves, and what we are all about. Death is there to allow that which is no longer needed to move on, and in doing so, create the space for that which is needed to replace it, so that we can move forward; this is essential. It is a critical part of the process, and to desire life without death is to desire life without life. Life in the absence of death is not life, it is something else. Therefore, trying to create a path that excludes death, is to choose a journey of avoidance, evasion and denial. The struggle many people have with this is simply another form of avoidance. We will be drawn to the books and the programs that tell us the struggle is not necessary, and there becomes a point in time when life becomes struggle free and without conflict. This too is a misrepresentation of the true nature of life. The struggle of death holds within it the seeds of new life. Source never removes without replacing something of equal or greater value, but we must be open to seeing it as such.

Nature Tells Us the Importance of Death

Simply look to nature and you will see life itself tell you how important death is. The most obvious example of this is the winter. This is a time when everything appears to die; everything goes to sleep. Winter is the moment in nature when the ground, the plants, the seeds, and life that the summer brought to us all go to sleep. It is the same reason we sleep, for a time of rest, cleansing, and letting go. Without the winter, spring is left without the refreshed and revitalized qualities it needs for the

148

birth of the new to happen. Death in nature is seen many times during the year. Each season is born and dies. The death of the season is what facilitates and allows the next moment to be as perfect as it needs to be; it is this death that makes way for life. Therefore, avoiding death is a conscious decision to avoid life.

Resistance: The Death of Death

It takes more energy, focus, frustration, and pain, to fight death. This way of being is the way of the fool, as death 'must be'. It is as present and real as the breath we breathe, whether we see it, accept it, work with it, or explore it or not. For those who accept life with death as a part of the package, the experience of self is much more significant. When we attempt to turn our back on death, we are simply facing a life of struggle and hardship that is unending, relentless and unforgiving.

The wise person is the one who embraces death, even with its changes, challenges, fears and power. Life and death are not separate, nor can they be selected as if they are a part of an a-la-carte menu. Death is the plate that the main course is delivered on. We are forever eating from this plate and all that we have in life has come from a death of some kind and will lead us to rebirth.

Do Not Be Afraid

Before we can come to understand the entire concept of death, there is much that can cause us to live in fear. This is because in our ignorance of it, we will create endless possibilities of thought in relation to what happens when death occurs. We may fear the percieved realities of it, the coldness, aloneness, suffering, pain, anxiety, being lost, not knowing, and the end of everything. A focus like this will create a real experience of imbalance, upset and stress. No wonder so many of us avoid even the subject of death and try to live as if it does not exist. Once we understand it, there is nothing to fear in the death experience.

While we are living in our ignorance of the death process and running scared every time it comes calling in some form, we are missing out on a truer and more authentic understanding of the event. We are missing the 'experience' of letting go, and we are losing out on the awakening that comes with that experience. Ultimately, we are preventing our experience of the rebirth and evolution. When we try to hide from death, we are learning nothing about understanding it, and seeing the glory that exists in allowing this essential element of life to happen according to its own true nature. Like everything in life, death brings us a gift. It is unwise to reject it and live in denial, just because we don't like the wrapping the gift comes in.

The Gift of Freedom
Whenever we feel we have to run from anything, we are not free. If we are in avoidance of our own true nature and we cannot find the qualities within us to face our fear, we are not free. When we are living in such a way that the very nature of life is blocked from touching us, we are not free. When we are not free, we are in a constant struggle that can only be resolved by turning around and walking into the issue itself.

If we were to use the Christian analogy of heaven and hell for a moment, it will soon be clear as to why so many opt to remain in pain rather than choose freedom. For now, let's use the analogy that freedom is heaven and pain is hell.

--Heaven exists at the far end of hell.
--To get to heaven you must go through hell

Translation:

--Freedom exists at the far side of the pain.
--To get to freedom you must go through the pain.

The pain that is being referred to here includes all of those things within us that keep us separate from our true nature. If you are familiar with Christianity, you might see this pain as being similar to what they refer to as sin, which is a falling short of the mark or being distant from God. It is that which keeps us from ourselves, that which keeps us from knowing that we are God, a small portion sent here to know and experience the powerful truth of who God really is. Therefore, we are all one.

Pain can come in many shapes and forms, but in the end, it is neither good nor bad, right nor wrong. It is only an experience. Pain is the experience of separation from the self. It is ignorance in knowing our true nature, and blindness that prevents us from seeing that everything is connected.

We must allow death to become a part of our everyday life. We do this by letting go of the old, allowing room for the new birth; this is the very thing that brings freedom. This freedom can be seen and experienced in our individual lives as follows:

--We have total control: we soon realize that we have the power to create our reality and there is nothing to be afraid of, not even death, irregardless of it being emotional, psychological, spiritual or physical in nature.

--We have no fear: when we are free, we are living in confidence, knowing and consciousness. A person with such abilities and learned skills does not live in or from fear; they live in and from allowing and thus, peace. This does not mean that fear is gone from life, it simply means they know what choice to make when fear shows up.

--Be open to accepting the gifts: the freedom of life serves by allowing us the grace of trust; it is from this truth that gifts are given when they are needed.

--Creating possibilities: all things are possible. When we come from the field of potentiality, our potential is found in the silence of a free mind. The mind that lives in fear is always too busy to allow silence.

--Empowerment: who we are fully opens up and blossoms like a spring flower, when we have the space and the experience of being free. The empowerment of this alone allows us to continue traveling the spiral of life without questioning the journey, and simply allows it to be what it is.

--Deep understanding of life: the freedom that is afforded to those who choose that path brings with it the gifts of wisdom, knowledge, healing, confidence and teaching. It also enables us to become our best student and at the same time, set an example for others.

--Closer to our true nature: a free person has the vision and the insight to see that everything is connected and all is perfect just as it is.

The Invisible Connection
Why it is so difficult? Think of a man presenting you with a bag full of snakes; asking you to open the bag and take the snakes out. I guess my initial response would be along the lines of 'forget about it, if it was just one snake I might try it, but a whole bag full, is not going to happen'.

It is for the same reason, that moving through the hurts in life can be so difficult. Seldom do these hurts come one at a time, but often they come in what appear to be bundles; some that we can vividly recall, some are sketchy, and some that we have no sense of at any level. There are even occasions when some of these so-called burdens are not even our creation, but the inherited pain of the family lineage.

Since everything is connected, when we are going through some form of drama or trauma in life, we are also revisiting the other times in our life that our experience was similar. We are often not aware that this is happening.

The only way to create a reality where this is not the case, is to go through the pain, experience the healing, and free ourself from the prison of fear. Let's use a relationship breakup, as an example. When a breakup is especially difficult, and we can't seem to find a way to manage it, it is most likely due to the fact that we are experiencing more than just that relationship breakup. If we have had previous relationship issues that remain unresolved (no closure), it is likely that we are still experiencing the emotions that were involved, and they have become magnified. It is like "Oh, no, not again!"

It can go much further than that, a relationship breakup may trigger trust issues, for another person an insecurity, for still another, it may trigger both trust and insecurity. Knowing that these issues are not limited to relationships of the intimate kind alone, it is likely that we are going to experience all situations and unhealed hurts from our past that in any way involved trust and insecurity. So, our relationship breaks up and we are feeling let down; our trust has been broken. These feelings awaken all other moments of similar experience in the past regardless of the nature of the relationship that created the feeling. The relationship breakup could awaken the pain of a difficult father relationship, the hurt from the betrayal of a business partner, the memory of an abuse as a child, and/or the feeling of depression that followed a time of financial difficulty.

All of a sudden we are facing a bag full of snakes and not just one. It seems tough enough to try to get one snake out of the bag, no wonder we run from the challenge of taking them all out and untangling them in the process. Too many teeth looking to sink themselves into your skin, better to close up the bag and lock it away. Therein lies the problem. What about the next time we experience something that hurts? All these snakes awaken and this time they are as they have always been, only now they have another of life's moments added to the mix. Until we finally decide to face them, the hurt will always be there. Remember that pain is allowing the death of something in order to allow for the new. Yes, it can be scary, even difficult. We may feel like we can't do it, and there may even be a moment of total collapse in the midst of the untangling, but that is the nature of death, and that is the nature of allowing it to be what it is meant to be.

Once we are in the process and allowing death, (as if you can do anything about it anyway), we will realize there is little to fear. Without taking the time to fully explore the concept of death and one's self in relation to death, how can we ever master our feelings about it? One of the greatest gifts available to us, is the gift of getting familiar with how death feels and allowing it to be, without needing to change it. We just need to learn to ride the dragon, or simply be, it depends on your perspective and the need you have while allowing the experience. Most importantly, we must remain focused on the fact that death is a daily reality, and is not limited to a physical death at an old age, or any age, for that matter.

Engaging in 'The Process' of Life and Death

This is something that can be talked about at length, but only understood from experience. The process is not difficult to do, but doing it can require us to go where we have spent our life trying to avoid it.

1. Take a moment in silence to allow yourself to connect with your body.
2. Scan your body and observe your thoughts; do not attach to them, simply notice them.
3. Find the feeling or the thought that is nagging at you.
4. Focus on the feeling, and ask yourself 'what is this feeling connected to'? If it is a nagging thought, ask yourself how that thought makes you feel, and begin with point four again.
5. Catch the first thing, person, memory, feeling or circumstance that comes to you. Trust that it is connected.
6. Do not try to understand what you are seeing, feeling or thinking. Simply observe the experience and as you do that, allow yourself to release anything that is connected to it that is causing you pain.
7. As you release your issues, other images, thoughts and feelings will come up. Repeat the exercise with each of them.
8. During the healing process, many emotions will arise. Allow them to come up. If you feel the need to cry, just

cry. Don't judge the tears, simply allow them to happen. If you feel vulnerable and scared allow that too, they are all a part of the process. Whenever an emotion comes up, repeat the exercise with each of them.

It is always good to do an exercise like this in a place where you will not be distracted. Outdoors in nature can be very powerful, but if you are indoors, you can create an environment around you that is complementary to what you are doing; light a candle, play some soft music, burn some incense and if you can give yourself some time after you have finished the exercise to relax and re-enter your body as much as possible before trying to get back into your day. For a few days you may feel the emotion and the healing. Allow this to happen in as gentle an environment as possible. Avoid attempting it where possible arguments, cross words, judgements and upsets in general may occur.

Don't be afraid to let death in, it brings with it only new life.

Engaging in 'the process' of seeing death as the creator of life

1. Identify an issue or challenge in life that has caused you to feel hurt, angry, upset or broken.
2. Allow that memory to rise up within, but do not see it as who you are, simply observe it.
3. What change did it bring to your life?
4. Where did it cause you to go and what did it cause you to do?

5. What good came from that change in where you went or what you did?
6. What was the lesson learned?
7. What has come into your life now because of that change, no matter how small you feel it is?
8. Write out that memory; only this time make it a positive memory and call it, 'The life that death brings'.

Contradiction # 9

Responsibility Happens When You Are Not Responsible

Your job in this world is to evolve into the best version of you that is possible. It is your task to move beyond the apparent limits in life to discover the true essence of what life is. It is your calling (from within yourself) to meet the challenges of life, and learn how to overcome all levels of resistance. How you experience life while on that journey is entirely up to you. That experience is determined by the choices you make, the actions you take, and the perception you choose to have in relation to your life.

It seems to me that many people do not fully understand what it means to be responsible. It is not unusual to see people acting from a place of 'control', thinking they are just being responsible. Many examples of this can be seen in parents as they raise their children. They often control the child's life by making choices for them, or passing on beliefs that they are attached to, without actually considering the child or the true impact the beliefs may have on them. This control can come in the form of a judgement, a criticism, withholding information, or even in stretching the truth.

We can also see these forms of control in schools, although teachers and authorities often do not see it as control, but 'acting out of responsibility'. Control can be seen when a child is punished with detention or extra homework; it can be seen when the child is told to walk, not run. It can also manifest when school staff contributes to a consciousness of believing that good people are clever people, and success in life depends on high grades.

It is not unusual to witness a form of 'control' in intimate relationships when the partners think they are simply being responsible and loving. Not enough people realize that it is not our job to change the other person in a relationship. We are there simply to love them as they are, where they are, and with no agenda other than to live from that love so that evolution can happen.

Many of us go through life feeling that we are responsible for those around us and believing that, without us, these people would potentially suffer, get lost, lose their meaning and purpose, have to do with less, be sad, miss us, and have to struggle through the rest of their lives as if a piece of them was missing. We believe this so profoundly, that we have created an incredible web of stories to support it. All of these stories are entangled with each other to the point that they hold each other up, support each other, and offer a level of credibility and credence to each and every other story. All of this keeps us from understanding the real purpose of life and relationships.

In most cases, these stories are nothing more than ego scripts, long-winded psychological convincers, that make us feel like we have a purpose, a place, a meaning, and a worth. You may be thinking, 'Well of course, without people and situations we are responsible for, what is the whole thing about, and who am I?' Our stories and scripts of responsibility give us a label, an identity and a context for our lives. Of course, these are important to most people, so it is wonderful to find something (someone) who can provide all of those things.

It is an illusion to think that these people we feel 'responsible for', lead us into our core reason for being. They become the answer to the question, 'Who am I?' If you allow yourself to grasp this concept, you may begin to see the reason that people fight so fiercely to hold onto their identity. Unfortunately, they will do this, even if the fight brings them to a place in life where they are miserable, upset, disempowered, alone, frightened, or even dying. There is a conversation with self that is going on at a subconscious level that says, 'It might be killing me, but at least I know who I am, so I am not letting go of it. I will fight to the death if I have to'. You may find this difficult to believe, but if you stop for a moment and look at the world around you, you will see many examples of this. Perhaps even in your own life:

> --Look at the couple in the middle of the break-up, each fighting so hard to hold onto their identity, that they do great damage to each other. One fighting to hold onto the illusion of the identity of 'spouse' or 'partner', and the other fighting frantically to hold onto the identity and label of 'freedom' or 'independence'.

--Consider a religious organization, and how it fights to hold onto its labels and identity of authority, even after the world has turned its back on it, and evolved to a new level of consciousness. It uses judgements, shame, humiliation and guilt, as tools in the war of disempowering others, just to hold onto the illusion of power.

--Think of the manager in the company who will bully and intimidate others, just so they can continue playing in the illusion of their position, label, and identity. This makes them feel like someone with a position in the world, a place where they can be respected.

--Think of the parent who punishes a child by shouting at them because they got something 'wrong', made a 'mistake', asked the 'wrong' question, spoke out of turn, or refused to do something that the parent wanted the child to do. Imagine that a parent will shout at the child they claim to love just to show who is in charge, just to make sure they hold onto their label, identity and purpose.

The power of the label, the significance of an identity, and the magic of a purpose, are spell-binding. So much so that we can often forget what matters most, and get lost in the ego trip of being 'someone'. Life may become a little easier if you begin to believe that you are either 'everyone' or 'no one', but I would recommend that you at least start to lose the idea that you are 'someone'.

Perhaps it is time we begin to let ourselves off the hook. Yes, we are wonderful, but no, the world doesn't depend on us to keep going, and every other person in the world has the same abundant potential that we do. They can and need to do it for themselves. Hold onto the 'nothing', and start being responsible only for yourself. Let nature guide life at this level. We will only find the strength and the resources to focus on the self and act out of responsibility, when we stop burning up all of our energy and resources on trying to be responsible for everyone else.

The following is a beautiful story. For me, it speaks of allowing the world to be just as it is, and allowing ourselves to be just as we are. Everything is enough, just as it is. It may not make sense to you, but who said it was supposed to make sense? The day we stop being responsible for the world, and allow ourself to go on our own journey, is the day we have taken the greatest leap toward peace and abundance. It is the day that we begin to trust that everything is capable and able. It is a whole new level, a whole new journey, and a whole new us.

The Story of the Butterfly
(Author unknown)

A man found a butterfly cocoon. One day, a small opening appeared. He sat and watched the butterfly for several hours as it struggled to squeeze its body through the tiny hole. Then it stopped, as if it couldn't go any further. So the man decided to help the butterfly. He took

163

a pair of scissors and snipped off the remaining bits of cocoon. The butterfly emerged easily but it had a swollen body and shriveled wings. The man continued to watch it, expecting that any minute the wings would enlarge and expand enough to support the body. It never happened. In fact, the butterfly spent the rest of its life crawling around. It was never able to fly. What the man, in his kindness and haste, did not understand was that the restricting cocoon and the struggle required by the butterfly to get through the opening, was a way of forcing the fluid from its body into the wings, so that it would be ready for flight.

Sometimes struggles are exactly what we need in our lives. Going through life with no obstacles would cripple us. We would not be as strong as we could have been, and we would never fly.

Building an Attitude of Trust

We can move beyond the struggle and begin to experience a different level of life, one that doesn't overwhelm us, when we begin to build an attitude and mindset of trust. This means that we begin to see beyond the fear that someone or something is out to get us. It means moving past the concern of losing everything we have worked so hard to accumulate. It means seeing something great in every situation. I once heard someone say that great things can come from the worst experiences. At this point in my life, I have to agree that this is very true.

An attitude of trust means that we learn to step out of our comfort zone. It means realizing that we may *feel* lost at times, but trusting in the knowledge that we can never really be lost. A life of trust means accepting that what happened in the past was then, and this is now.

Trust is something that involves all of who we are. It reaches places far beyond the thinking mind. When someone experiences a moment of fear and lack of trust, there is thinking involved and also a high level of emotional and physical stimuli present. It is the interaction of all elements of the self that create such a surge of power in moments like this. Therefore, it is fair to say that growing beyond, moving into, and evolving past issues with trust can be quite difficult.

Building a life of trust does not mean that we begin to let our natural defense barriers and protection systems down. It does not mean that we trust everyone and everything; it simply means that we get to know, communicate, and contract with ourselves all that is required, in order for us to trust our own judgement. In doing this, we will rarely, if ever, need to look beyond ourselves to know the best thing to do in any given situation. This 'trust' building is something that we will be doing for the remainder of our lives. We can certainly create a life experience that allows us to move beyond the painful points of learning how to trust. In essence, we will always be learning how to trust, as trust has many levels and many dimensions to it. As soon as we have one mastered, we will be brought through the comfort and into the next level of learning. The journey never ends; it is a continual process of learning, growing and moving deeper within. Remember, life is about growth and learning, so we can't expect life to stop existing as itself. In other words, we will always be learning and we will forever be seeking. The only difference is that with time, we begin to develop expert skills in relation to the process, and it becomes a different experience each time. The battles will continue, but at that point, we are conscious and a lot of the time we are living from a state of being, as consciousness itself.

The Joy of Being Selfish

You can't get through life without playing your part in all of the relationships that come your way. It is your job to interact with other people, places and situations in such a way that you empower them, and at the same time, inject them with the realization of oneness and connectedness. However, in order to be fully responsible to the world, there first needs to be a moment when you go within, and become fully responsible to yourself. You will never bring anyone or anything past the point that you have not brought to yourself. Therefore, in order to be responsible for others, you need to put yourself first. This is not selfishness in the 'negative sense'. Instead, begin to realize that there is a positive and powerful aspect to selfishness, and you are being called to embrace it.

Don't Take Yourself So Seriously

Most of us often take ourselves too seriously. We forget to laugh at ourselves; we become convinced that life is a serious matter. Sometimes we live as though the idea that too much laughter means that we are being immature. We get upset when things don't work out as we thought they would or should. Fear ofen takes over when we think that we have done something wrong. There is a need to control everything so we can get all the necessary pieces of life into the right places at the right time and in the right order. With no sense of humor, an over-inflated ego, a fear-driven motivation to get things right, and a memory loss in relation to what matters most, we are asking for trouble, and trouble is what we certainly get.

When we are taking ourselves too seriously, it is because we think we know how things need to be, and we are busy trying to make them that way. In doing so, we forget that we really know very little about anything. We forget that life is a gift, and laughter is a tool that keeps us young. The truth is that allowing everything to be just as it is, ensures that our stress levels remain low. Accepting things as they are does not mean that you give up your dreams, or your desire for change, it simply means that you approach change from a conscious state of mind and not a place of activated turmoil and conflict.

Not taking yourself so seriously will ease the burden of thinking you need to have an answer for everything. It will ease the need to be right all the time, and it will put a significant dent in your need to blame others for your misery. You will no longer need to be seen as smart, intelligent, ahead of the game, or in charge of everything all the time.

So what are you doing when you are not taking yourself too seriously?

--You are taking time to stop and smell the roses.

--You are smiling a lot and laughing more.

--You are asking powerful questions about life and creating more space for quietness and peace.

--You are not suffering from so many physical, emotional and psychological issues.

--You do not become depressed as easily. In fact, you are starting to believe that depression doesn't really exist, and it is only a state of consciousness that is a choice you make.

--You are working in a job that doesn't feel like a job. In fact, it looks and feels more like a hobby.

--You are in love with yourself and the world.

--You are giving thanks.

--You are breathing deeper.

--You are making decisions for yourself.

--You trust your own judgment.

--You are more focused on the needs of those around you, and because you are in a powerful place of self-awareness, you are teaching the world to do the same, just by being you.

--You are not reacting to outside events; you do not allow yourself to believe that they have any control over you.

--You are sleeping better and looking forward to getting up in the morning and embracing your day.

Believing in Others

While we continue to learn about the power in the above attributes and take ourselves less seriously, we will not be able to avoid the reality of other people in the world around us. As our perception of ourself changes, the perception of others will change too. We will begin to believe in the people around us from a place within us that assures us that it is safe and is to be celebrated. We will see things in people that we have never seen before, like their qualities, capabilities, gifts, similarities to ourselves and their wonderful differences. Our attitude about the nature of people and the future of the world will change; it will become more positive as time passes.

Instead of seeing life as a path we must walk alone, we will begin to experience the path of life as one that is full of support systems, loving people, encouraging words from strangers who seem like friends, and we will realize that there are people who actually want to see us succeed. Our life journey becomes one of love, possibilities, support, encouragement, positivity and success. Furthermore, the days of aloneness, anxiety, loss, pain and failure begin to fade into the distance.

In order to hold on to this new experience of life, and in order to build on it, so it grows stronger each day, we simply need to continue doing what we have been doing to get there in the first place. Continue processing and continue to let the healing in. Keep taking risks and know that we can trust every moment. At this stage, the worry of 'things not working out' has left our life, because we now understand that even if things do not work out, everything is as it should be. We are starting to live in a place of 'knowing', and the confidence that it brings takes care of much of the worry, stress, and anxiety of being lost.

All of this change will happen because of the change within you in relation to yourself, and will have little to do with any external factors. It will seem that those around you have changed, but in fact, they are most likely the same as they were yesterday and the day before. You are the one who has changed, and therefore, how you *see* them has changed.

If I Feel It, or See It, It's Mine
There is a mighty phrase in the world I live and work in, that makes me laugh every time I hear it. It takes the power out of judgement, it stops assumptions, and it creates a moment where thinking is required and reaction to default habits is limited. The phrase is:

'If you spot it, you've got it.'

It would be wrong to suggest that you take this phrase literally in every sense all of the time, but in essence, you can use its theme, tone and intention; the results can be fantastic. I am suggesting that whatever you see in the world around you is only brought to your awareness because a vibration, the same as the vibration of that very thing, lives within you. This is true in relation to people, environments, situations or feelings, beliefs and perceived realities.

Think for a moment about someone you love, someone who inspires you, someone you might say is a hero in your eyes. This person can be a public personality or someone closer to home; someone you know personally. What is it about this person that you admire and appreciate so much? Name the qualities that stand out to you in this person?

Let's say you said any of the following qualities: passionate about life, loyal, honest, compassionate, forgiving, gentle, optimistic, positive, respectful, etc. The only way you can know and identify these qualities, is if you also have them. How else could you identify compassion if it is not first living within you? Surely, if you did not have compassion you would not be able to identify compassion for what it is. It would stand to reason that if compassion is not something that dwells within you, you could not have the language of compassion or the knowledge of what compassion is, in order to identify it in the first place. I know there is the argument that a person could be identifying compassion in another from an intellectual perspective, and they are simply saying what their logic suggests the observation is. However, it is not my experience that this is so. On most of the occasions that I have worked with clients in this context, we have found that the person does indeed, have that very quality within them. It is often a lot stronger and more prevalent than they may have originally thought.

Why does it work this way?

Possibility 1: We see things and people that connect us with the possibility of accessing this quality and learning to release it, understand it, and live from it.

Possibility 2: All things are connected and we are now evolving into this awareness. Life seems to have a powerful way of making great miracles seem ordinary, in order for us to continue exploring and searching.

Isn't it a beautiful thought to think that you have within you, all the qualities you admire? It is a wonderful realization, to know that I am: passionate, loyal, honest, compassionate, forgiving, gentle, optimistic, positive and respectful.

'If you spot it, you've got it.'

However, take a moment and think of a person you do not get along with, someone that upsets you and makes you feel very uneasy, unsettled, sad, or maybe even hurt. What is it about this person that makes you feel that way? Name the qualities of this person that stand out for you. Perhaps you see them as: devious, hurtful, angry, bitter, negative, selfish, ignorant, unbalanced, greedy, egotistical, etc.

How is that working for you?

Perhaps you see a certain person in your life as ignorant. How do you know they are ignorant? Does it not stand to reason that the idea of knowing you're compassionate, because you can see it in the world around you, supports the idea of you knowing that you are also ignorant because you see ignorance in the world around you?

There is no doubt that there is truth in the saying, 'If you spot it, you've got it'. However, I do not encourage you to take it literally, it has many levels of truth to it that only show themselves to you as you practise seeing life as a mirror of your own reality. It is like everything else in the world. It requires you to process it in relation to your map of the world; how you live; who you say you are; what you believe, and the idea of evolution and growing beyond the experience of life you are currently dancing with.

With this in mind, let's try to answer the following questions:
--What does compassion (or ignorance) mean to you?
--What is it about compassion that you admire?
--How does compassion speak to you? What does it say?
--What are the dreams you dream when compassion is alive and well in the world?
--What does compassion represent to you and for you?

Take it a step farther...

Once you have answered the questions (of course, you can change compassion for a quality that you truly connect with), take your answers and meditate with them for a while. This does not require

173

any experience or training. By 'meditation', I am simply referring to you being mindful of the answers.

Once you have spent a little time on this, answer the following questions:

--What, in my life, needs compassion?
--What is the hurt that I live with, that is asking for compassion?
--How can I be compassionate with myself?

Do this also with the 'negative' qualities. Ask the questions in relation to ignorance, and then, after you have taken the time to be mindful of the answers, consider the following questions:

--What am I being ignorant of in my life?
--What positive benefit has being ignorant brought into my life? What has ignorance protected me from?
--What mindfulness do I need to develop in order to be less ignorant?

On the journey of learning the art of responsibility, you cannot bypass the importance of caring for the self. In order to truly care for others, you need to love yourself more than you have ever dreamed, thought, imagined or believed. The challenge is one of learning to know what it is to love yourself, and then to experience that love with all of who you are. Once you can do this, you then need to make this experience of love your way of being in every moment of every day. It is a way of life.

You cannot be responsible for another, until you are first responsible for yourself. Of course, we are speaking of this in the context of consciousness and having a positive, growth-based experience of life. I say this because it is possible to be responsible for someone else, and still mess it up beyond measure. It is this reality that has brought the world we live in to the level of darkness, madness, pain and destruction that we witness every time we listen to the news.

Being 'Response-able'

You are always '*able*' to respond to your life situations and moments. There is never a moment when you do not have the capacity to choose and respond. This brings us back to earlier chapters when we highlighted the reality that you are the one in charge, and your day is the consequence of the choices you make. Your choices are your actual responses.

Finding the confidence within to know that you are response-able can be a challenge, if you were not brought up in a world that encouraged free thinking, self-awareness and conscious living. Somewhere within every one of us lives a spirit that has the strength, courage and confidence to stand up and be counted.

The Price Paid for Responsibility

Living from a consciousness of responsibility can be nothing less than peace-filled. How could we not have peace, if our life is focused on taking care of the entity that we are. When we are loving ourselves, we are navigating life with an awareness of all that really matters. We are living from a 'heart space' of doing what serves us best, doing what serves those around us, and doing what serves the world.. Being responsible involves being of service to the world, and knowing that, is essentially our reason for being.

We live in order to grow into the best version of ourselves, and as this best version of the self, we love those around us so they can grow into the best versions of themselves. In taking part in this dance, we are assured we will leave this world in peace.

When we accept responsibility for our life, we are saying 'YES' to:

Love
Peace
Fulfilment
Life
Death

The Price Paid for Peace

Once we are sitting in peace, there is nothing that can disturb us, that is, other than a decision to move out of peace. Consider it this way; once we are being at peace there is nothing else, only peace. It will remain so, as long as we continue to accept it. Even getting to that place can be a powerful experience, if we decide to become the peace we are seeking.

The only price to pay for it are the things we give up, in order to allow peace to be our way of life. Here is a list of some of the things we will no longer be if we are being at peace:

Angry	Lost
Lonely	Alone
Sad	Depressed
Judgemental	Dishonest
Anxious	Afraid
Hurt	Addicted
Sense of lack	

Celebrating Me

Behind all the words, under all the hidden suggestions, and within the different attempts to open our mind, there is only one message here: celebrate life! To celebrate means to rejoice, have fun, party, enjoy ourselves, launch the boat of life, and live our life in such a way that we cannot avoid knowing we are alive.

How much do you celebrate your life? What are you doing that is fun? Or do you take it all very seriously? Do you know how to party? Can you dance? Are you playing it safe or are you stepping out of the boat and walking on the water? Are you dreaming of something or someone in your life; or are you just sitting and wishing, thinking and trying to affirm it into your life?

To celebrate life requires your active participation in all aspects and moments, regardless of what is happening, and regardless of it appearing to be 'good' or 'bad'. Think for a moment of a great birthday bash to celebrate a 'Sweet Sixteen' or a 'Twenty First'. At this party there is plenty of smiling, lots of fun and games, friends interacting, and talk of the life journeys that lie ahead.

There is good food, great wine, and a real sense of being in love, or a zest for life. There is an inner peace and an outer radiance. As you celebrate you, you are teaching the world to celebrate too. Why would you choose anything less than making every moment one of celebration?

Engaging In 'the process' of being responsible by not being responsible

1. List all the people, things and situations that you feel you are responsible for.
2. List all the things you are responsible for in relation to that person, thing or situation.
3. Identify the reason for your belief that you are responsible for the things you have listed.
4. Identify who or what taught you that you were responsible for these.
5. What do you think being responsible gives you or does for you?
6. What would happen if you allowed life to take over and guide these things, instead of you being responsible and controlling them? Remember, if you do not consciously make the choices, it will be decided for you.
7. What do you need in your life that you feel you do not currently have?
8. How can you give yourself the answer to #7?
9. How can you give yourself the things you answered in #5?
10. Are you ready to let go and trust?

Contradiction # 10

Imperfection Is Perfect

To some, the world we live in and the life we have in it, is a beautiful design filled with powerful moments of self-realization and meaning. To others it is simply something that needs to be 'got through'. It offers more pain than love, more debts than abundance, an imbalance of opportunity, and a constant demand to get things done. The reasons for such a contrast in experience could be *blamed* on many things, but essentially it boils down to a few simple matters. Once we know what they are, it is easier to understand that it is all about one powerful but very simple reality.

What is Perfection?
First and foremost, perfection is a judgement and one that comes with quite a punch. The idea that something is perfect suggests that something else is not perfect. After all, what do we have to measure perfection against other than the things that are not perfect? The idea of achieving a state of perfection as a person, is of course, not based in reality. It places so many demands on a person, that all they see, notice and become aware of, are the things that need to be 'fixed' in order for them to be 'right' enough to be accepted. Accepted by whom and for what reason?

This need to achieve a state of excellence, faultlessness, exactness, and precision is, without a doubt, the single most powerful negative force any of us faces. At one point or another, everyone has been frozen by the power of its coldness and held to ransom by the brutality of its demands. The greatest power of the illusion of perfection is the fact that so many people believe, without questioning the belief, that a state of perfection actually exists.

Like everything else in life, perfection exists, but not as you might think. Perfection is found in allowing everything to be just what it is, as it is, and seeing that it all makes 'perfect' sense. It exists when we accept life without the need to change it. There is perfection when we embrace ourself, without the thought that we are not good enough. It also exists when we are seeing, with intention, the connection and meaning in everything within us, around us, and because of us. By allowing this, we are open to seeing that the imperfection of life is already perfect and nothing needs to be changed, saved, restructured, cut down or controled.

The Few Simple Matters
When we become lost in the need to strive for perfection, we are:
1. Feeling the need to achieve a state of validation from an external person
2. Suffering at the sound of an inner voice that says 'you are not good enough'
3. Struggling to see the greatness in ourselves that we see in those around us
4. Trying to make up for past mistakes

5. Under the influence of the need to control everything in our life
6. Unable to live in or are unfamiliar with the idea of uncertainty
7. Living from a feeling of powerlessness
8. Striving to prove that we are right and someone else is wrong
9. Reacting to an unknown inner reality that says we are wrong and need to make things right

The Powerful but Simple Reality

All of what we believe 'matters', doesn't really matter once we can see the force that is behind each issue. What lies behind each issue is the need to control, in order to create a certain reality. What is the reality? The desire to be accepted.

The ultimate influence behind the need to control is 'fear'. Where there is control there is fear. As sure as night follows day we will always find within our moments of needing to control, the power of fear, the preacher that fear is, and the uncompromising starkness of the fear. Fear takes no prisoners, it comes with an emotional, psychological and physical force that has the wherewithal to knock down even the strongest of people, unless they learn what it takes to understand and dance with it.

Fear can be connected to many things, of not being accepted, not being good enough, not having an answer, and thereby being ridiculed or labeled as stupid. Fear tells us that certainty is the only cure. The problem with this is that the capacity to control

181

everything all of the time, the seeking of perfection, and the idea of certainty itself, are all illusions of life that have been taught to us by a system of authority that lives in fear. These words are the language of the masses that do not see life as their's to manage.

We have been given the opportunity to break free from what we have been told and what we have allowed ourselves to believe. The real goal is to find out how to let go of certainty, control and the need for perfection, when they are the very things that are keeping us from reaching our full potential. However, beginning with the idea that everything is perfect in its imperfection is a powerful starting point.

You

There is nothing about you that is not beautiful and powerful. There is nothing you need to change. You are perfect just as you are. This does not mean that you are without what you might refer to as blemishs or flaws; it simply means that you are perfect as you are, including the blemishes and flaws you chose to see, find and label. They are a part of you, they make a significant contribution to who you are, how you are, and the reason you give yourself for 'being'. You are a living and breathing miracle. The world within your body is a constant experience of incredible and awe inspiring events. Think of the amount of muscles, cells, tissues, bone and information that is involved in just clicking your fingers. This happens the instant you think the thought and give the command for it to happen. In that very second, thousands of realities kick into being and create the result you commanded.

There is nothing about you that is anything less than wonderful, amazing and beautiful. However, you may not see that as your reality. Be careful of your thoughts and beliefs, least you create them negatively. It is true that you get what you focus on. Can you see any connection with how you see yourself in the world, and how you are actually thinking about yourself?

--When did it all start to go wrong?
--Where did you first begin to feel that you were not good enough?
--When did you first start to dislike yourself?
--Who told you that you needed to be something different than who you are?
--What is the perfection you are chasing?
--Do you know how truly sad it is that you don't love you, that you can't hold yourself?

There is a significant game that is being played out within each of us. We say to ourselves that we are not good enough and then believe it. However, when we say to ourselves that we are beautiful, somehow we cannot seem to believe that.

What Do You Get From Imperfection?
It seems that we only allow into our lives the things that serve us well. To most this sounds like a crazy statement and it would be no surprise to hear someone respond that it is rubbish. What is it about being hard on yourself or believing that you are not good enough, that is serving you well? Each of us have to answer that question for ourselves, but you can be sure if you believe it, there

is something inside you that is telling you it is good to believe it. In believing it, you are saving or protecting yourself from something that may hurt you. The amazing thing is that believing it hurts you as much, if not more, than anything else could or would hurt you.

What is the need for perfection (that sabotages your efforts) giving you, that makes YOU feel you need to hold on to it?

> --Is it protecting you from confrontation?
> --Keeping you safe in certainty, even though it hurts, as uncertainty might hurt more?
> --Getting you the validation of the people around you who think they are helping you by keeping you focused and striving for more?
> --Giving you a place in the world, or with the 'right' friends, that makes you look good?
> --Distracting you from the true calling within that you simply don't understand and therefore avoid?

It Not A Job for the Head

As is the way with most things in life, the understanding of how imperfection is perfect, comes from experience, and not logic. The logical mind will allow you to challenge your old beliefs and maybe even begin to put a real framework around the new concepts. However, it is true understanding that comes from the wisdom of experience. It is the difference in grasping or understanding it, and knowing it within you. When you have knowledge of these matters, you can talk about what your head knows, but your head can never know the emotional, psychological or spiritual aspects. Your head needs information that seems solid and rational in order to converse about such things. However, when you actually experience it, that experience informs the mind with the knowledge, wisdom and understanding of all elements of your break through (or experience). It is then clear to the point that you can talk about it beyond a normal level.

Its All About the Heart

The intelligence of the heart is what we need to access the experience and understanding of life. We will reach the point of knowing that nothing needs to be changed. Our heart has as much, if not more, brain power than the brain itself. Furthermore, the heart can speak the languages that the logical head has yet to learn. Our heart will deal with all that matters; it deals with the experience and the feeling. It does not get distracted by the judgements of life, the detail of a story, or the fact that something should be different than what it is. When we work from a heart space, we are allowing the most pure, uncompromised and authentic element of the self to take charge and run the show. The heart is not concerned about getting it right, it simply gets it. The heart is not influenced by others in its decisions; it simply knows its job and does it. The hearts job is all about love, acceptance, allowing, healing, opening, nurturing and holding. These are the very things that are experienced when we begin to seek out the journey of knowing that everything is perfect just as it is, even in its imperfection.

Living with and from the heart is a full time commitment. We need to allow ourselves to discover the nectar of the heart and drink from it until we are heart drunk. Allow the power and the pull of the heart to be your teacher, your guide, your friend, your lover and your inspiration. There are no half measures in the world of the heart. Once you have taken the journey in that direction there is no going back, and once there, you will be consumed by all it has to offer.

You are perfect as you are, as you are *is* you. This perfection in you is real, whether you believe it or not, makes no difference. However, there is a significant difference in how you will experience life, depending on your belief or lack thereof, as a perfect you.

Engaging In 'the process' of seeing perfection in the imperfection

1. List everything that is good about you.
2. List all the achievements in your life (no matter how small).
3. Identify all the moments in your life that you laughed.
4. Identify all the great ideas you have ever had.
5. List all the feelings you have ever felt that helped you or another person in a moment of difficulty.
6. Go for a walk in nature and look around you. See how beautiful it is. See all the crooked lines, uneven surfaces, contrasting colors, plants that are dying, trees that have fallen, things that are broken. See how beautiful and

perfect it is, how it all fits together, and creates a flawless and beautiful image.

7. Recognize this image as a reflection of yourself.

Contradiction # 11

The Answer Is,
There Is No Answer

There are more than six billion people on this planet and most of the time many of these people go through their average day in accordance with certain belief systems. These beliefs act as filters and all information passes through these filters. It is all a part of the process of coming to a conclusion about any given issue. Of course, conclusions are good because they provide answers that give a sense of knowing and certainty. As we know, 'certainty' has a powerful hallucinogenic quality that makes us feel that everything will be okay, even if our reality says it is not. The illusion that we choose to believe IS the reality that matters most to us. We will do whatever is needed to avoid living in fear of poverty or death.

Our beliefs are constructed to create 'order', to 'control' situations and people, and to make sure that the systems of right and wrong, good and bad, are unhindered and thus, they remain masters of our fear. Who created these fears? Unfortunately, the lessons we were taught through our parents, church, teachers and friends, to name a few. Of course, we also created them; you and me. Most of these constructs direct us down certain paths in life and use emotional coding to ensure that we stay in line and don't become independent or self-reliant. If you take the time to look closely at most of your beliefs, you will discover that they are ridiculous, and lack any sense of real meaning. Most of them don't even make a contribution to the world in a positive way. In fact, they are likely to be detrimental to the world that we want to create at a number of fundamental levels.

I hear more and more people in recent times asking the following questions: Who *can* you trust anymore and what has it all been about (life so far)? Unfortunately, most people who ask them don't take the time to sit with the questions and try to fully understand what it is they are asking, let alone make an actual attempt to answer them. If you look closely at the questions and scratch beneath the surface, there are many things being said:

I am living without direction.
I am lost.
I am afraid.
I am without security.
I am disconnected.
I am without true relationships and leadership.
I am confused.
I am worried.
I don't know what the point is.
Do I have a point and a meaning?
I am tired.
I need help.
I need answers.

The truth is, you already know the answers

All of the answers to your life's questions already lie within you. Furthermore, within you exists the source of creation itself. There is nothing that you do not know and nothing that you cannot navigate. The key is to become aware, to waken up and to realize that you are 'it'. The idea of this awakening is easy to get your mind around, once you make the decision to make your life a conscious act of 'being'. With this commitment comes a flow of inspiration, information and experiences that will be reinforced as you walk farther and deeper into the self.

There is a consciousness within you that knows you are God; it knows what you are capable of; it knows what you have achieved so far, and it knows what you can achieve in this moment. However, in your conscious state that the information is presented to you, you do not yet believe this, and therefore you are distant from your own true nature. You do not accept what it is that you *truly* believe. You are not yet allowing yourself to fall into your authentic self and live from that place.

There is no amount of thinking in the world that can give you the understanding required for you to grasp this. The missing piece is the 'experience', and from the experience all of the blanks are filled in. All that which seems broken is understood as perfect. The experience is the key, the path to follow, and the way into the self. The experience is you and you are the experience. All that you are and all that you have will change many times, at many levels, on the way to being at peace with the self. When you arrive at this place called home, your world will look like it has always looked but nothing will be the same. You will be the same person you have always been, but you will be entirely new and nothing will be as it was.

You already know this inside; now you must start believing it and experiencing the belief.

Being 'Not Enough' is Enough

There is nothing else you need to be other than yourself in this moment, in order to activate the deeper level of self. By saying, 'be yourself', I may be asking a lot. Let's go back to some of the questions asked throughout this book so far:

--Do you know who you are?

--Have you any idea why you are here?

--What has it all been about?

--Have you learned the lessons and experienced the moving on, or are you just living with a lot of logic and book learning?

--Do you talk about what you have learned but nothing seems different inside or out?

--Do you know that you are God?

--Can you grasp what it means that you are God?

--How much of your life is given to meditation and contemplation?

--Can you hear the inner voices and tell them apart? How many voices are there and what are they saying?

--Who is in control of your life?

If you cannot sit with these questions, it is going to be very difficult to enter into that place called *nothing* from where all things come, and where all knowledge exists. Here is the good news though; all you have to do to begin moving inwards is to sit with these questions in deep contemplation. You never need to answer them. In fact, it is futile trying to answer them. The answers only exist in the experience we talked about. Once you experience the self, all of these questions will be answered. The answers will just be there as if they were always there, and guess what? They always were.

Just as you are today is perfect enough. Don't try to be something or someone you are not. The more you try to have the right answers; the more you try to control by saying the right things and creating the right impression. The more you try to avoid getting it wrong (which is not possible) and the more you do what is needed to 'keep up appearances', the further you move from where you want to be.

You are enough right now. There is nothing for you to be other than yourself, there is nowhere for you to be other than here in the present and there is no time for you to be other than this very moment. Again, everything is perfect right now. This perfection is not going to change. However, you can affect this moment by choosing to 'not see' the perfect order in the chaos, the perfect blend in the tapestry, and the 'perfectness' of you. Stop trying and just 'be'. Notice I didn't say 'do', I said 'be'.

Even though you may not believe that you are enough, there is a voice within that will confirm this is so; that is, if you become silent enough to allow it to speak, and then allow yourself to hear it. I know that you do believe this at a true and authentic level.

192

Now you simply need to connect the different parts of you together, so that you can believe every day. Then you are almost home.

The Elusive Perfection

Perfection is the sense of everything being without flaw, blemish, or brokenness. It is an illusion that things need to change, grow, develop or evolve into something they are not. There is no perfection in that context. Those beliefs will simply distract you from the really important work of experiencing life.

Let us take a moment to remind ourselves that everything is as it is, and it is perfect that way, even if it seems to have flaws and imperfections. These flaws and imperfections are simply human judgements. Remember too, that they were formed through filter systems; these are connected to beliefs that were imposed on us by someone else. More than likely, that someone was 'doing their best', but they too were under the control of others, and in fear of the 'systems' that were in place at the time. They too, were certainly not living life as an experience, but as a list of things to do and achieve.

My purpose here is to assist you in opening your mind and heart to the fact that we are perfect just as we are right now. The only thing that gets in the way of our experiencing ourselves as perfect is our inability to believe it, although deep down we know it is true.

Close your eyes for a moment and persist through the resistance and you will experience that knowingness. Once you have experienced that one brief moment, all you need to do is follow the same path and increase the number of short moments of authenticity you have. Soon you will have decreased the amount of time between them. Before you know it, you will be living from a confidence and a purposefulness that you once only imagined.

You know in your heart that there is more to you, more to life and more to this whole experience than meets the eye; you also know at some level that it is undeniable. Now you need to search for the part of you that will allow you to fully accept and believe it and live from that belief.

There is little else to do.

There is nothing only this moment.

There are no answers.

There is nowhere else to be but here.

You are everything.

Death is beautiful.

Life is the doorway that leads to death.

Death offers the understanding that you are alive.

The entire journey of *YOUR* life is one of *YOUR* making. What's more, there is no 'one' journey. The possibilities of how to experience life are endless, truly infinite, and you have lived each one of them already. Everything that could be, has been or can be has already been. You are simply choosing to experience this version of living now and in this manner.

In summary, the following few points may help you to gain some clarity and move forward by learning how to stand still and be in the moment where you are.

--Your life is primarily a spiritual journey with human experiences intertwined.

--Learning how to understand the human experience will help you to manage the non-human elements of self.

--The purpose of your life is whatever you say the purpose of your life is.

--There is no God in the clouds with a beard and a list of who is good and bad.

--You are the expression of God, the breath of God, the experience of God and that which God knows itself to be. You are God.

--Money cannot buy you happiness, but it does help in a world that sees it as an essential tool for playing in the game of life, and there is no shame in it.

--It is better to live with nothing for a while, in order to experience everything.

--All that you see around you is an external expression of your internal reality.

--No one else is to blame for your life; you are where you choose to be right now.

--Yes, you are hurt and that hurt is powerful.

--Your pain is not a negative, but a powerful and positive learning experience.

--There is a way through and a way out and it exists only within you.

--Institutions offer nothing to you but imprisonment.

--Peace is the only thing worth seeking.

--Peace brings with it freedom.

--Life is not what it seems.

--You are not free when you think that you are responsible for people or things, nor are you allowing them to be free.

--Your discomfort is there because you know sorrow, and the reason for the sorrow remains alive within you.

--Healing happens, but asking for it is often futile. You must become the healing itself.

--Looking for peace by creating a debt-free existence will not bring you what you seek. What you seek is much more than freedom from debt.

--Looking for peace by finding the perfect relationship will not bring you what you seek. What you seek is much more than what you can find in another person. You will find it within you.

--Looking for peace by trying to get rid of your worries and stresses will not bring you what you seek. What you seek is much more than you can find in the idea that you have no worries or stresses.

--The journey is one of self-discovery and that journey requires you to move beyond the realities that hold you in your current reality. You are already there. Remember, everything is already in place.

The only place to be is here, and the only way to be here is to stop the fighting. The fight will hold you in the past and the future but it will never allow you to be in the present. Find within you all that is needed to break free from your struggle. All you need is already there to be unleashed. You are everything you need to be, right now.

In order to be that which you dream of, you must surrender to who you really are. You are God. Many people spend a lot of their lives worrying about who they *have been* and not enough time experiencing who they *really are*.

Engaging In 'the process' of realizing there is no answer

1. What is the answer you are looking for?
2. What will having that answer give you?
3. How can you give that to yourself without having an answer?
4. If you knew for sure that no answer existed what would you do?
5. Take action on your answer to number four.

Contradiction # 12

The Truth Is
There Is No Truth

If we were to gather together all the people of this world who have a specific belief about the 'truth' in relation to who we are, where we are from, and the concept of God, how many truths would there be? Quite a few, I would guess – tens, if not hundreds of thousands. That being the case, which one of them is RIGHT?

I was brought up believing that there is one God and one faith. This God was the creator of all things and nothing existed without him being its creator (yes, he was a man, very definitely masculine and there was no question about it). Of course, when someone would show themselves to be different to the demands of this faith, they were labeled, ostracized, given the cold shoulder and in many cases, simply side-stepped as if they had wandered off the path. You were either a follower of this God who could give you the knowledge to find out what life is all about, or you were in his bad book or on his bad side. Everything else you might have believed in was a false god and was punishable by humiliation, shame, guilt and fear. God was the head of a specific religion and that religion was the only doorway with access to this God.

When you are seeking an experience of life that is free, honest, authentic, and focused on enlightenment, there are a few things worth noting:

--There is no one truth. Everything simply is what it is. Everything IS the truth for the person experiencing it.

--God (if you choose to use that word) belongs to no religion.

--There is not just one way to access the life force that some call God. There are many ways, and for each of us, a very different, unique and appropriate way.

--For you to access the Divine source does not depend on any one person dying, suffering, rising from the dead, walking on water or turning water into wine. You can access the Divine source because you *are* the Divine source.

--Living according to one truth limits your options in life, and cuts off the potential to discover other paths to the same reality.

--If the path you are following causes you to feel guilty, anxious, humiliated, fearful, ashamed, or dependent on an external party to get you there, you may be wise to step off that path and sit in the field for a while. The journey of discovery of your truth can be enjoyed, if it is a part of your bigger picture, your dream.

--What is a truth for you today may not be a truth for you tomorrow. Truths change, and sometimes daily, as we grow.

--Truth is a concept of the mind and has nothing to do with anything worth focusing on.

The whole concept of truth isn't confined to the religion, faith and God discussion. The idea of there being 'no one truth' extends itself into all sections and areas of life. It is so in relation to financial matters, relationships, health, politics, career, family and anything else you wish to attach it to. There is no 'one truth'. I am going to list a few of these in more specific terms below to give you an understanding of what I mean. You may sit easily with some of these, while others may not be able to get through your thinking at all. Just because you don't see it doesn't mean it isn't there. Do your own research and let that research begin internally.

--Governments think that there is one way to 'rule' a country and that is how they do things. However, there is no need for governments. There are other available options in life rather than the government systems.

--The land does not belong to you, you belong to the land.

--It is not true that you have to pay your mortgage. Mortgages, private loans, credit lines and all other financial 'debts' do not really exist and are not necessary. Of course, if you don't do your homework, if you do not tap into the wisdom within, if you do not separate yourself from the game, you will not be able to see how this is so, and you will continue to play life by other people's rules.

--You do not have to work in a 9-5 job in order to generate the resources you need to live peacefully.

--It is likely that many of your family and friends are lost, clueless, and unable to help you constructively on your life's journey. You don't need to take their advice in relation to what you should do, how you should do it, what is right for you, and what the truth is. Your truth may not be their truth, and vise versa.

I could list one issue after another here to highlight all the different things in life that are typically managed with a 'norm', as society has learned to believe that the norm is the truth in relation to how things get done. Remember, all of life is not as it seems. There is no 'one truth'. In fact, the only rules in the game of life are as follows:

--Do no harm to yourself or others.

--Take nothing that isn't yours.

--Do all you can to help others discover their true self, purpose and meaning (in other words, help people find their way home).

--Love who you can, whenever you can.

--Allow the world to love you.

--Live in consciousness and know that you ARE consciousness.

Once I make sure to check in with these things in my life, everything is open for discussion and all possibilities are considered. There are no limits, no restrictions, and no negatives. From this place, I make the decisions that allow me to live from what I know to be a Divine flow, a Divine energy and a Divine confidence.

Don't Work, Just Play

There is no need to take life too seriously. So many people believe that they need to get up and do a job in order to get by in life. When you challenge this, and tell them that they don't have to, they are armed with one excuse after another to prove that they do: 'I have to provide for my children', 'I will have nowhere to live if I don't keep my job', 'That's the way life is', 'I have no choice', 'I just grin and bear it'. There are so many programmed responses, and so many codes built in, that people conclude that 'life is a certain way', when, in fact, that is not necessarily the case. However, once the 'truth' has been triggered, everything else is a distant possibility, and it takes a lot of hard work to get someone to give it any consideration. Just to remind you what the truth is -- there is no truth.

I am continually amazed by the people who participate in my programs. They turn up coded and conditioned, with all they need in order to 'know' what they need to know to survive and play the game of life according to their truth. Many of these codes are so ingrained and entangled with so many other truths, that even they can see that change is nearly impossible. However, after only a few days the change begins. Why? Because they discover that the truth is not THE TRUTH, but simply 'A' truth.

Truth = Reality

There are many truths and many realities. The main objective is to lose the need to use either word and live each moment consciously and label-free. That way, all things are possible and you are free to experience all those possibilities.

Don't take life, yourself, others, jobs, money or anything else too seriously. I'm serious, nothing is serious! Learn to make life a game that you play. That doesn't mean that you do not respect, love, appreciate and cherish life. It simply means have FUN and *go with the flow.* Create your flow and create your fun. Perception is the key.

There Are No Pockets in Your Shroud

Live each day like it is your last. What is the purpose of living in such a way that you store up wealth? Pardon the pun, but the old adage of saving for a rainy day just doesn't hold water. When you finally 'kick the bucket' you won't be able to take any of it with you, as there are no pockets in your shroud. Spend everything in your life, let everything circulate and live knowing that whatever you need you will create, and therefore, will have it when it is needed. If you allow yourself to live this way, and you make it a default way of being, you will never need to worry about the rainy day, for when it comes, you will be living in a world where you create what you want and need, when you want and need it. You will never be without.

All things that come into your life are meant to be circulated. Nothing is designed to be held onto. Everything must be allowed to keep moving. As it moved to come into your life, it must be allowed to move and pass through your life. Nothing escapes this. The need to accumulate things, wealth and possessions is a product of cultural thinking that is not serving you well.

In the ideal experience of life, you will be able to live in peace, with peace and from peace, but if you are always looking to gather things 'just in case', you will not be experiencing peace too often. You are continually distracted from the peace by the search. If you do get the things that you think you need, you will simply spend your life worrying about losing them, or worrying about the resources running out. You will never have enough as the nature of the gathering mindset is to keep gathering. That is the way the game of truth works.

--It is the 'truth' that you need things so you spend your life looking for things and, no matter how many things you get, you will continue looking for more things as you continue to play this 'truth' over and over in your head.

--It is the 'truth' that once you stop gathering things, the resources you have stored away will begin depleting so you keep on gathering.

--It is 'true' that to be happy you need a house and to have a house you need a mortgage. Therefore, you do all you have to do in order to get the mortgage in order to have the house. You are so caught up in the truth that says 'house = happiness' that you don't stop to think that the mortgage will be a rope around your neck for up to 30 years, and until you have it paid off. Unfortunately, you can't be all that happy because you are stuck in the new 'truth' that when you have the mortgage paid off you can relax and begin to enjoy life, because the pressure is off.

--It is 'true' that money has a real value and, without it, you can't have any decent kind of life. So you give up all opportunities for a decent kind of life in search of the money that will truthfully bring you a decent kind of life. The only problem is that it doesn't work out... ever.

--It is 'true' that when you meet the right person, you will be happy.

Are you beginning to get it? There is no truth, there is only experience and experience teaches. Jesus is not the truth; your spouse is not the truth; money is not the truth; Buddha is not the truth; the church is not the truth; your dream is not the truth. THERE IS NO TRUTH, that's the truth.

'THIS STATEMENT ON THE NEXT PAGE
IS ABSOLUTELY TRUE'

'THIS STATEMENT ON THE PREVIOUS PAGE
IS ABSOLUTELY FALSE'

In-Summary

Everything is a Reflection of You

It seems to me that if you were to choose to see everything as a reflection of your own reality, you might be backing a winner. I have lived this way for some time now and every day I am given insights that exceed my own personal development and spiritual awareness. In effect, what I am doing in choosing to see that everything is a reflection of me, is choosing to take responsibility for every moment, every experience and every situation I encounter. It doesn't really matter who else is involved or what is going on, I am willing and able to see what it represents for me and within me. The benefits of this are too many to mention here, but I can promise you this: As a result of living this way, I have discovered the secret to creating a life of peace, love, abundance and freedom.

The dream I now live is far beyond anything I could have imagined for myself before setting out on my search. By seeing everything as a reflection of myself, I learned about me, who I really am, what my capacity is, and the authentic nature of what it means to be me. I discovered that I am not my name, I am not my job, I am not my words, I am not what you say I am. I am free, I am. In the beginning I would get hung up on seeing someone very angry, or blaming me for something that was an issue in their life, but in time I began to understand what it meant to see everything as a reflection of me, and from that the discovery came.

One summer day I was driving along the coast of Ireland and I stopped to look at a tree that was in bloom; it was beautiful. The color was rich and the tree was tall and strong. The green and golden fields that surrounded the tree were beautiful; the horizon was powerfully defined and the blue sky was deep and mesmerizing. As I stood in awe, I began to lose my mindfulness of what I was experiencing. I was simply lost in the beauty of what I saw. The experience was about the feeling and not the vision of what I was seeing. As I drove along the road after having this wonderful moment, I began to think about the experience and wonder how amazing it would be if I could feel that way about ME. I thought it would be fantastic, that is, if I could experience me with the same intensity. Right away, my thinking mind began to throw obstacles in the way of this ever becoming a possibility, and most of these thoughts lead to the same place: 'The scenery was perfect and nature is perfect, but I am not perfect, so I could never see me with the same eyes'. I don't know what triggered the next few moments of inspiration, but out of nowhere came a rational voice, the echo of reason, and it began to speak to me about how imperfect nature is. Here are some excerpts from what I heard.

> 'Don't be daft, that tree was full of crooked lines and broken branches, it wasn't perfect at all...but it was beautiful'.

'The horizon...it was no different than any other horizon...but still, it was beautiful'.

'The fields might have looked beautiful and romantic, but if you walked through them, you would be covered in mud up to your neck...but they were beautiful'.

This voice continued to speak to me about how imperfect everything was...but how beautiful it was at the same time. As this dialogue was going on, I finally stopped the car. Something had happened, the proverbial penny had dropped, and it was a lot bigger and heavier than I had expected. I immediately turned off the ignition, found myself a comfortable position in the seat, and closed my eyes. I acknowledged that I was there (in the quiet of my mind), and I tried to feel what that thought would feel like if I expanded it beyond just a thought. I went into the feeling I had when looking at the scenery a while back, and consciously transferred the feeling from the scenery to me. I began to allow myself to accept what I felt was the fact that I was filled with flaws, but beautiful nonetheless. I felt I was cheating a little by using the feeling that belonged to the scenery for myself, but I soon got over that. I had the most amazing sense of love and appreciation for who I am, and where I am from. It was one of those blessed moments when things that were always floating out there with seemly no answers, began to make perfect sense to me.

The formula was quite simple really. I was experiencing a feeling and followed that feeling until it showed me where it was relevant in my own life. As this happened, there were so many other things happening at the same time. I was given a look into the deepest part of my life and shown what was there to be healed, loved, appreciated and honored. I was shown only what was authentic, and the feeling that existed during these moments was a feeling that lasted long after the experience. I discovered from this that feeling an experience is much more important than understanding the experience. It makes perfect sense now: Experiencing love is much more important than understanding love; experiencing peace is much more important than understanding peace; experiencing beauty is much more important than understanding beauty; experiencing life is much more important than understanding life, and experiencing me is much more important than understanding me. The irony is that once you really have that experience, all of a sudden you understand and you realize that the understanding doesn't matter all that much in the bigger scheme of things.

No matter what you come up against in your life, detach from the external experience and journey inwards with the feeling. This is where the teaching and the wisdom are, and it is within your own self that all will make sense. You will soon discover that nothing really exists as you once thought.

Nothing is Something

One day when I was in my twenties, I was sitting on a bar stool with an old frend. I am not sure what was going on for me at the time, but mid-conversation I stopped him and said, 'You know, nothing is something'. He looked at me over the top of his glasses, laughed from his belly, and said, 'That's enough drink for you tonight'. However, something inside me had just awakened. I knew I was on to something and what I had just said made perfect sense to me. Not only that, but I had a whole world of concepts attached to that statement that I wished to explore.

It was a lonely time, really, as there were very few people, if any, in my life with whom I could have these conversations. This guy was the best of them, not because he engaged in the philosophical discussions, in fact, he rarely engaged, but because he would just sit there and listen. I was in full exploration mode at this time in my life. Others at the time would dismiss the conversations as drunken chatter and change the topic to issues that 'really mattered' in life: football, who bought what, who works for who, what woman just walked in, and so on. Don't get me wrong, I was interested in all of that too, but at the time, I was beginning to move into a very different experience of life.

So what did I mean by nothing is something? In essence, I was thinking about the fact that there is a whole lot of space in the universe with what appears to be nothing in it, and what a waste of space that seemed to be. At the same time, I was becoming aware that if there was a whole lot of nothing there, that nothing was just as significant in the universe as the something that is in the universe. The very fact that the significant nothing is there and is a part of the universe must be something. Although I have no idea what that meant (not sure if I do now either), what I was beginning to grasp was this:

--Nothing was there in the beginning.

--Anything that exists now came from the nothing.

--Nothing is something that has an incredible creative power.

--Nothing is the place where silence exists.

--Silence exists between all the noise.

--The noise comes from the silence.

--Nothing and silence are one.

--Nothing and silence create everything.

--Nothing is everything.

--Everything is nothing.

--All there is, is nothing.

For me, life is all about finding the 'no-thing' and resting there. This means sitting in the silence and, without judgement, allowing all that 'is' to be. When we are in this state for sometime:

--We become detached from all things and all people.

--We experience the self at a very different level.

--We detach from all labels, names, understandings and coding.

--We will then experience the self and observe the experience.

--We are no longer trying to get things right or make things fit into place.

--When we allow ourselves to 'be', everything is perfect, just like the country scene I spoke about earlier. The state of being in nothing is the most valuable goal to set for yourself.

On our journey to this state, we will go through many levels of self, and will be given the instructions necessary to learn, grow, understand, accept and immerse ourselves in the spirit that we are.

This experience cannot be understood in words, but needs to be experienced, and it is there for all who wish to seek it. It is, after all, simply an experience of the self at an authentic and honest level, one that is accepting and non-judgemental.

Dancing with Ego

The only thing that prevents us from having a wonderfully authentic experience of the God that we are, is when we get in our own way with our thoughts, beliefs and concepts of true, false, right and wrong. These are the ego games that we play due to our life coding and conditioning. They are also a part of the natural dance of life in the context of learning, growing, discerning and navigating our individual path to personal freedom.

Our ego is a part of who we are, and for that reason we do not want to cut ourselves off from it. I have heard many people advise others over the years to detach from the ego. I suppose it sounds like a wise thing to do, but I could never understand how it could be wise to cut off something that represents so much strength, power, capacity, willingness, determination and cunning ability. Instead, I traveled on a journey of understanding the ego, loving the ego, learning from the ego and taming the ego. I never intended to cut off from it, only to know it and love it. Today, I am great friends with my ego. I let him dance his dance, make his moves in life, speak his words, and sing his songs. In turn, my ego rests for me while I travel within to be still and rest in spirit. While I travel in the meditation, contemplation, and experience of 'being' peace, my ego bows and respects its creator. I have learned to play with ego and to allow it to play with me. However, I have a solid agreement from deep within myself that I am to be attached to nothing, to depend on nothing, and to bring nothing into my life that I am not willing, ready and able to leave when the time, circumstance and moment is best.

When I was in the very early stages of learning to master the spiritual self, I became aware of the trouble my ego caused in my life. There were a few powerful desires and outcomes that I was attached to, and I attached to them with all my might.

> --I longed for validation; I wanted to know that the world around me recognized me and loved me.

> --I longed to belong; I desired a place to call home where I would be heard, recognized and could be sure that my place at the table of this home would always be there.

> --I craved affection; there was something within me that knew I was carrying a significant level of pain at an emotional level. I knew that learning how to give and receive affection was a key component to the healing required.

Here is where the ego became a significant issue. When listening to the voice of 'want' within, I thought that if I received validation, belonging and affection from the people and things in my life, I would feel the wholeness I was seeking. After many years of seeking this, I was left with many great hurts, disappointments, losses and experiences of brokenness. It was only when I began to listen to the voice of 'need' that I began to realize what was missing. I knew that all I needed was peace, and once I had that, there was no need for anything else, even though everything else came with the peace. It was from this place of awareness that I learned how to dance with the ego, how to feed it, how to calm it, how to love it, and how to allow it. It is my motto--not to deny any part of who I am, but instead to celebrate all of me with the greatest possible love I can find within. The trick is to learn to do this in the context of fun and learning, while remaining detached from the details and the 'shiny' things.

The Leaders are Just Being Pushed

You need no system, no government, no church, no school, no guru, no medical system, no legal system, no corporate system, and no financial system to find peace. In fact, these things will prevent you from being free, and peace is only found through freedom. In order to break out of the prison of being stuck and being lost, we all need to realize that a new way of living is required. A new level of consciousness is waiting for you to tap into it, and from this consciousness you can have it all: peace, joy, abundance, happiness, love and understanding, meaning and purpose. This consciousness knows that systems and leaders are not needed anymore.

We give way too much credit to those who are in leadership roles in life and those who we elect as governments. We live from the assumption that they actually know what they are doing and we need them to do what they do or we will lose out and achieve very little. For some reason, we believe that they provide essential parts of what we need, and without their presence in our governments, schools, local communities and legal systems, we would be unable to move forward. The reality is that all of these 'leaders' are being pushed to do what they do by situations and factors outside themselves, and most of these situations and factors are corporate-connected, money-driven and selfish in nature.

With few exceptions, those in government don't care about you, don't know you, don't want to know you, and don't want you to contact them. You are simply the excuse they use to do what they do, which is to take care of themselves and their illusions of grandeur.

Would it not be foolish to allow your life to be motivated, moved, inspired or encouraged by a system that lives from such a different set of values than yours? Perhaps you are a die-hard optimist and you believe that anything is possible; that change can happen among the leadership. Well, I would suggest that you take all that optimism and powerful belief, and use it to create a new way and let the old way die. Remember, it is all about birth and death. If we are to allow the new to live, we must make a contribution to allowing the old to go through its death. This contribution, in some cases, is to stop breathing life back into that which needs to die, if the flow of life is to run free once again, perhaps for the first time ever.

The Sanity of Madness

Taking the steps needed to change our experience of life and live our dreams, will demand that we go against the normal flow of life. The decisions we make, the places we go, the way we speak, the questions asked, those we connect with, and the way we spend our day, will all change significantly. The changes that people notice in your life may be so unexpected and so out of the 'norm' for them, that they may even wonder if you have lost your mind. You might say, well yes I have; I now operate more from the heart. If this happens, you are on the right track, so keep going!

If you are seeking to change your life and nothing is changing, then you're missing something very important. I would suggest that you stop and rethink the situation. The nature of change is change, so don't think that you can get there without the change happening. The greater the change, the more likely it is that you are doing what is necessary. Always remember to check in to make sure that the change is aligned with your higher values, purpose and desired outcome. Always check to make sure that spirit (the authentic self) is providing the majority of contributions and input.

There is nothing sane (few actually do it, the rest just talk about it) or normal about living your dreams and tapping into your deepest self. If it was normal and easy, everyone would be doing it. If you think you are mad, other people are telling you you're mad, or you are beginning to see signs of madness setting in, well done, you are well on the way to sanity. It is just that we have learned to call it mad, because it is not the norm.

The Language of Prison

We speak as we think and our thoughts create our reality. This can become a 'prison of the mind'. When you catch yourself using language that is negative, defeating, upsetting, angry, anxious, hurt, blaming, judging, disempowering, dark, slow, divided, uninspired, monotonous, colorless, or limiting, you are seeing signs that you are stuck in a prison of the mind that is not allowing you to experience life beyond the boundaries that you have built (or that have been built for you). The language of prison is very straightforward and it's all about not being able to move, being stuck, feeling the need to escape, wanting to expand, being protective and possessive, fearful, watchful, paranoid, and in denial. Many of us spend most of our lives in one prison or another, without even knowing that it is our reality, and thinking that we are free. We are given a few toys in life to play with; we can move from one place to the next, and so we conclude that we are free. In reality, we are prisoners of the systems that need and want us to remain stuck, in order for them to continue the illusions and build their wealth. Until we allow ourselves to wake up and claim our freedom, we are prisoners of:

--The government/political systems.
--The education systems.
--The legal systems.
--The financial systems.
--The medical systems.
--The corporate systems.
--The family systems.
--The societal systems.

--The religious systems.

If you think you are not under their control or being influenced by them, think again. Take a long look at your life, and you will be able to list entanglements so significant that it will amaze you just how much you are caught up and imprisoned, without even knowing it.

Freedom of mind, body and soul is the only escape. Create a life that does not depend on any system. The best way to do this is to learn how to love, accept, understand and allow death to happen. Remember, it is all about the death of old ways and the birth of new.

The Prison of Language
As much as being in a prison brings with it a language, it is true that language itself can bring with it a prison or freedom. Be sure to listen to the language that the world around you uses. In doing this, you will begin to see patterns of how and why life is as it is. Language, or words, are one of the most powerful tools used to create the reality in the world we live in. Think of the power of a sales person to sell you something you don't want. Imagine the power of the priest to create fear in the person hearing the sermon. Visualize the power of the president who reassures the people and creates inspiration. See in your mind the overwhelming power of the words of a judge in a court of law; they are so strong and powerful that they can put you in jail for life (should you give them jurisdiction over you). Now think of the power you have in your life to make things happen, stop things from happening, or

create excitement or joy. Imagine the freedom you can create in your world by speaking the right words and using a language of freedom.

All of those who have received some acclaim in life as a leader and/or a person of inspiration, have used language to share vision and change the world for better or for worse.

The language you default to will create your reality. Is your language creating a reality of imprisonment or an experience of freedom? There is no one responsible for your reality but you.

You are free – do you really get what that means? Maybe it is time to go a little deeper in your search and ask some new and powerful questions of the world around you.

Observing the Observer

A really effective way to learn about yourself, and then apply the learning to create a new experience of life, is to become an observer of yourself as you move through life. We have touched on this before, but it is worth mentioning again. When you can watch your actions without judgement, you are free (mindfully) to explore other options and possibilities, in terms of how you could behave in a similar situation in the future and yet get a different or better result. You are free to observe what happened before and what patterns exist. You are free to observe your psychological, physiological, spiritual, and emotional interactions, and see what the observation (judgement) says to

222

you about who you are, how you are, what you need in your life internally, and from the world around you.

However, it is also a good idea to take some time on occasion to observe the observer. That is, to observe yourself while in the process of observing. This will allow you to take an objective view of how you learn, what you resist, what you deny, how you ignore, and what reactions you make manifest. The different elements of yourself seen through the eyes of you, as an observer, will be ones of learning and growth.

We have a wonderful toolbox of hidden mechanisms that allow us to deal with all the stuff life brings. At times we think we are moving forward, when all along we are simply giving ourselves something to keep the observer happy, while we are deflecting the real issues that are required to create the real change. The whole idea here is to learn how to outsmart yourself so you can catch yourself avoiding you: the real and authentic you.

These skills can be learned and will change your life from the very second you learn them. Find the support you need and learn how to uncover all of the layers of the self that have become your protection, but are no longer needed. Remember, the only way out is through. No book, no audio program, no course can do this for you. They can only offer insight and encouragement, but the change comes from the change, and that only comes from the action.

Go easy on yourself -- but go into yourself.

Engaging in 'the process' of realizing that there is no truth

1. What are the judgements you make about life and people every day?
2. Is that true about both of you or just you?
3. Where did that judgement come from?
4. In believing that you are right, what is it doing to the other person in order for you to be right?
5. What would your life be like if you stopped making judgements?
6. Do you allow yourself to realize that judgements are nothing other than a way of being certain in a world that evolves from uncertainty?
7. What are the judgements you want to stop making about yourself and others?
8. What do you want to replace those judgements with?
9. Start acting out of the answer you gave to number eight.

On A Personal Note

Although writing *Contradictions* was both fun and easy at one level, it was quite an intense journey of healing at another level. The healing that is written into the chapters and exists between the lines is responsible for it taking those eighteen months and not three weeks, as mentioned in the beginning. Each contradiction is written from a memory of a life experience. I allowed the energy of that life experience, whether joyful or painful, to enter into the moment and do the writing for me. As this was happening, I allowed the healing to replace all other feelings. Each time I finished writing, I was filled with a joy and a level of magic within, and I could feel the healing power of life flow through me.

It was my intention to be as honest and as real as possible. In doing so, it is also my sincere hope that you will sense the safety and the authenticity, and they will become your guardians as you allow your own life moments of struggle, pain, and discomfort to come up and claim their healing. Although this book was written for you, it was also a gift for me. Writing each word on each page was a ritual of letting go and experiencing life lasting healing. I have worked on my own life's struggles and challenges in many ways for so long, and this ritual was the final step. This book brought me home.

An amazing and unplanned aspect of *Contradictions*, as she was being born, was the actual location she chose to come into being. I had intended to write the book at my then home, a small country farming village in Ireland. It is true that a number of pages did get written in that place of round stones and smiling faces. However, the book didn't seem happy to stay put in one place for too long. Together we explored many different places and eventually when she was finished traveling, she gently whispered, 'find me an editor, its time'.

The first piece came into being in Egypt, beside the sea and only a few hours from the pyramids. Here I wrote with great energy and an open compassionate heart. While there, I was healing all past relationship hurts, particularly the intimate relationships that offered me the opportunity to accept responsibility for my own life and my own decisions. These were the relationships that I thought once hurt me, and took from me the things I had worked so hard to find. I was acutely aware of the contradictions that exist in the realm of relationships and intimate partnerships. Connections I had hoped would set me free, but that so easily bound me to dependence more than independence; expressions and hopes for love that often offered me nothing more than a broken heart and rejection; the frightful moment of loving someone but not liking them very much; the feeling of being in someone's arms but being so lonely. Egypt allowed the space I needed for healing, and I charged this book with that love, that compassion, and that letting go.

Not too long after Egypt, I found myself sitting by a river in a small fishing town in Portugal. As I wrote, I was loving the part of me that was so hurt by the authority figures I had met throughout my life. I was loving the part that had gone into hiding when I was abused as a teenager; the part that was betrayed by his church so many times that I had stopped counting; the part that was so often taken advantage of because my high level of trust left me an easy target for those who feed on the pure of heart and the innocent.

This was a time of great challenge, and as I wrote, I felt deep within me the tears, the fear, the anxiety and stress of the boy who simply wanted to go to war and settle all the scores. I left Portugal very quickly, and without much thought, as the intensity of the pain was overwhelming for me. However, I returned and I finished the writing that needed to be done there. I allowed the healing and I charged this book with the power to breakthrough, the honesty to feel and touch the deepest pain, and the acknowledgment of how important it is sometimes to simply be in the feeling and not attempt to run away. Portugal was a mighty teacher and a great mirror for me.

A little further down the line I was writing in the window of a beautiful coffee shop overlooking Charles Bridge in Prague. Here I wrote with great joy, great romance, the feeling of endless potential, and with great possibilities coursing through my body. It was here that I learned to love the adult that I have grown to be, and I said goodbye to the child that so often needed to show up, bringing his guilt, responsibility and shame. Together we talked for many hours and an agreement was reached. This was a great moment of freedom for me after a life of looking for a way out of my inner prison and the coldness of judgement. I laughed and danced with Prague as we remembered her story of cold, heartless and painful years of shame and guilt. We set each other free and the pages of this book are charged with the power of that expression. They are filled with the invitation to grow beyond the pain, move beyond the shame, and eliminate the guilt once and for all.

Then it was time for New York and the inner call to accept the fact that I have within me every resource possible to achieve everything I came here to achieve; that which I am aware of, and that which I have yet to discover. The city that never sleeps brought me through a beautiful moment of touching the part of me that is ever watching, ever supporting, ever delivering, and ever growing. I charged the pages with the knowing and the assurance that I and you are enough, that we have what it takes and that nothing but our own fear, can prevent us from knowing life at the level of our deepest dreams.

It was while I was at my desk in Ireland, that I came to fully realize the extent of the healing and acceptance that I am one with all things; there is no separation. It was in those moments that the pain stopped being pain and became something else, something powerful, something loving and filled with goodness and opportunity. It was then that I began to live at a new level and was able to see life for what it truly is.

The journey of this book brought through joy and pain, aloneness and connection, peace and war. The details are no longer important. I live in the knowing and the knowing lives in me. Seeing and understanding the 'contradictions of life' are the greatest of all gifts. It is true that all is as it is, unless it is not.

My precious friend... you have never been forgotten and the entire universe is doing what it does in order for this moment to be what it is, in order for you to find what you are seeking, in order for you to meet your deepest self and in order for you to rest in the experience of your authentic truth...your battle is over, it's time to come home.

About the Author

Marcus James (McKeown)

A native of Ireland, Marcus curently live in Central America. He is a leading figure in the world of spiritual and personal development, and spends much of his time traveling throughout Europe, Central and South America & The United States..

For Marcus, there is nothing more authentic than to teach about freedom and sovereignty at an experiential level, all the while empowering those he works with to create the life experience they desire. His passion is in delivering workshops and programs that are focused on empowering people to discover their true potential. He is clear in knowing that we are born free, and freedom is the experience we are here to learn about, lose, and re-discover before finally coming home to the truth of who we are and what our lives are really about.

Printed in Great Britain
by Amazon

41025291R00129